Business is Beautiful

Beautiful

The hard art of standing apart

Authors: Jean-Baptiste Danet, Nick Liddell,
Lynne Dobney, Dorothy MacKenzie, Tony Allen

Graphic Design: Christoph Stolberg
Illustrations: Noma Bar

Published by:
LID Publishing
37 East 18th Street, 8th Floor
New York, NY 10003
United States of America

info@lidpublishing.com
www.lidpublishing.com

A member of:

www.businesspublishersroundtable.com

Printed in Spain

ISBN: 978-1-907794-39-1

Business is Beautiful

The hard art of standing apart

Jean-Baptiste Danet
Nick Liddell
Lynne Dobney
Dorothy MacKenzie
Tony Allen

Contents

Foreword

Jean-Baptiste Danet
CEO, Dragon Rouge

It's surprising how much passion you can find in the world of business today. And this book underlines how some individuals in business challenge accepted models of economics, statistics and rankings through their passion and intelligence in the way they lead and manage their organisations. It's more than just a straightforward entrepreneurial approach – these people have belief and goals that go even further. It's demonstrated in the way they behave and interact with people, inside and outside their businesses, and the creativity with which they fulfil their ambitions.

At Dragon Rouge, as a proudly independent company, this way of looking at business is important to us, and we like to challenge accepted thinking – so we wanted to pay tribute to these exceptional individuals who endeavour to make the world a better place through their businesses and their actions.

In considering the studies and league tables that are repeated each year, we began to think that there could be another way to see the world of business, among the surfeit of quasi-scientific discourse, prescriptive methodologies and measurement models. The freedom of being part of an independent, creative business allowed the idea to take root and grow. Being surrounded by strong opinions that fuelled new ideas, and working with talented people in an innovative company, created the atmosphere and the space to develop and articulate this point of view.

It was inside this atmosphere that the idea of Business is Beautiful began to take shape. The collaboration of a wide group of colleagues was a vital ingredient – lively debate, uncommon thinking, and analytical and critical faculties have all played a part in developing the core idea and the five themes that make up this book – it really has come from the heart of Dragon Rouge.

When we started this journey, we were looking for a way to capture this thinking, to demonstrate how beautiful businesses stand apart, and what it is that makes them "beautiful". For me, it starts with people, connecting at a human level, understanding that - whether we are a seller or a buyer - we should treat people inside and outside our businesses with respect and commitment, not judgment. That businesses should surprise and delight, entertain and encourage, be relevant and appropriate, and sustainable for the future through the quality of products or services that they deliver. We were looking for a different way to understand what makes businesses successful without resorting to yet another tool of exact measurement, to identify some characteristics that we can relate to in a more human way.

The extraordinary responses from the businesses we researched and chose to talk to have only reinforced our thinking and the core idea. Without exception, these businesses found it easy to recognise themselves in at least one, and often more than one, of the "Hallmarks" of beautiful business - integrity, curiosity, elegance, craft, prosperity.

Exploring these themes has been a rewarding experience. Our conversations with the beautiful businesses featured in the book have not only confirmed our belief, they've also taken us to unexpected places and revealed aspects of the nature of business that are still relatively unexplored. So we thank all of the brave pioneers who have taken part.

You can probably tell that I'm extremely enthusiastic about the ideas contained here; to me, it's a delight to know that the foundation of this book is just the start of our journey. It's a rich vein that we want to explore more - with the great businesses we work with, and with our whole team at Dragon Rouge.

Thank you for joining us.

Introduction

"Business or pleasure?"

Accepted wisdom tells us either that business should come before pleasure, or that the two should never be mixed. Business, it seems, was never intended to be pleasurable: the term originates from the Northumbrian word *bisgnes*, meaning care, anxiety, or occupation. Care is not a concept many people immediately associate with the world of work, but anxiety is certainly a popular theme. Particularly during an economic crisis. Business is easy to portray as a cold, unforgiving environment, where Joseph Schumpeter's "perennial gales of competitive destruction" relentlessly bluster, where dogs eat other dogs and where only the fittest survive.

But business isn't like this. Business is people. People who come together to achieve more than is possible individually. Achievement is easily measured through profit, but value is a much bigger concept. Beyond profit, businesses have the ability to make a valuable contribution to society. An MIT graduate channels his expertise to provide power to families off-grid in Tanzania. A doctor has set up a new model hospital to provide affordable healthcare in India. A man in Denmark has turned his love and compassion for his deaf wife into a business that helps millions, as well as making millions. The world of business provides countless examples of businesses that have achieved greatness; businesses for whom profit is a necessary but not sufficient condition for success. These are stories we believe we can all learn from. These are the stories that captivate us. These are the stories we want to share in this book.

The science of success

Admittedly, storytelling sounds a bit light for a book about business. Instead, we prefer to use a term like 'case study' to lend an air of medical gravity to the stories we tell about business. The management world loves to borrow serious-sounding language from the world of science. We talk about growth catalysts, market equilibrium, customer inertia, latent demand and business momentum. We apply statistical methods gleaned from science to extract best practice processes from business data. But is business really a science? Can the mechanisms that drive success be measured and translated into universally applicable principles and processes?

The history of business in the twentieth century reads like a case study in the effectiveness of a scientific approach to business. In 1903, DuPont introduced formulae for assessing Return on Investment, which heralded a shift in management style from the personal to the professional. Around 1910, Henry Ford became the first practitioner of "Just In Time" (JIT) production, which showed the world the potential of cost-efficient assembly lines. Towards the end of the century, W. Edwards Deming created the System of Profound Knowledge, which underpinned both Total Quality Management (TQM) and Six Sigma. In 1995, Jack Welch made Six Sigma central to his business strategy at GE and by 2001 had famously made GE the most valuable company in the world. The moral of the story seems clear: scientific methods make businesses leaner, more efficient and better organised.

But at what cost? The Deming System of Profound Knowledge can make pretty uncomfortable reading. The following passage is an excerpt from Chapter 4 of Deming's "The New Economics":

> The first step is transformation of the individual...
> The individual, transformed, will perceive new meaning
> to his life, to events... to interactions between people.

How many of us would willingly join a business that wants to transform us to the extent that our lives will take on new meaning? This is the kind of transformation we may expect to happen when we enter puberty, move in with a partner, or become a parent. It's not the type of change most of us would like to have imposed upon us by a business. Jack Welch may have created an immense amount of shareholder value, but in applying these principles he also generated significant criticism within the business community.

For the sake of balance, it's worth noting that GE's current strategy seems to have taken the company to a much happier, healthier place. "Ecomagination" is the embodiment of a new belief at GE: that an environmentally driven business strategy can benefit society as well as the bottom line. They may have a point. Since its launch in 2005, ecomagination has delivered US$105 billion in revenue.[1]

This raises a serious question for the science of management: does human happiness figure at all in these equations? Do intangible virtues such as creativity, passion, commitment or imagination play any quantifiable role in value creation? We've dissected the subject of business to death with the cold, dispassionate scalpel of statistical analysis. Advances in neuroscience have delivered insight into those areas of the brain that correlate with the emotions businesses seek to inspire in us: joy, surprise, desire.[2] But the inner workings of our hearts, minds and souls remain largely shrouded in mystery. We have done all we can to de-humanise business in our attempts to achieve scientific credibility. The scientific approach has undoubtedly created an improvement. But what are the limits of this approach?

The importance of unmeasurables

How will scientific techniques evolve to create more value in future? There only seem to be two possible alternatives:

> ➢ there are measurable drivers of success that management science has so far failed to recognise, either through lack of technology, investment, insight or imagination; or
> ➢ there are intangible drivers of commercial success that defy measurement.

The first option is a possibility. We are constantly creating new business models and management science will almost certainly need to evolve in line with these. But this has always been a game of catch-up: first we created factories, then we used management science to help us run them better. You can't analyse how to improve a process unless that process already exists. This is a critical weakness of the statistical approach: it can only identify incremental improvements. It's impossible to create radical future business models by analysing patterns in today's data. As Bruce Cameron stated in 1963:[3] 'It would be nice if all of the data which sociologists require could be enumerated because then we could run them through IBM machines and draw charts as the economists do. However, not everything that can be counted counts, and not everything that counts can be counted."

The science of business management suffers from another problem: you can only improve what you can first measure, and at least one member of the "management science hall of fame" has come unstuck this way.

Robert McNamara[4] was "the can-do man in the can-do-society in the can-do era." He had an MBA from Harvard Business School. He was the first President of the Ford Motor Company to come from outside the Ford family. He was President of the World Bank for thirteen years. He was also the US Defence Secretary who presided over America's involvement in the Vietnam war. JFK recruited McNamara to the position with a brief to improve the efficiency and effectiveness of the armed forces. In this position, McNamara shunned the advice of experienced military leaders in favour of systems analysis to make key decisions during the Vietnam war. With the benefit of hindsight, many of these data-led decisions proved to be fatally wrong. His life is like a case study in the potency of analytics... and its potential to misdirect and mislead. McNamara's legacy is a warning to anybody who wants to use only scientific approaches to make decisions where unmeasurables are involved. This legacy is encapsulated in what has come to be known as the 'McNamara Fallacy', the gist of which runs something like this: You begin by seeking to measure what is important, but end up only attaching importance to the things you can readily measure.

This is a significant issue for management science once we leave the factory floor. There are plenty of attributes relevant to business processes that we can measure easily enough. But there are also plenty of unmeasurables: for example, the need for creativity, enterprise and adaptability within an organisation. The problem for management scientists is that it is frequently the unmeasurables that make all the difference. Science has played an essential role in helping businesses to work better, but it's important to be realistic about the limits of analytical approaches. They can identify marginal improvements, but they aren't a source of greatness.

This book explores those unmeasurable drivers of success — few of the themes we discuss lend themselves to quantification, but they are difficult to argue against as desirable and valuable aspects of business.

The 'hard art' of business

So we return to the question at the start of this book: business or pleasure? Science or art? Professional or personal? It's tempting to think of business and pleasure as incompatible, just as it seems logical to think of art and science as antagonistic. But there's really only one sensible approach to the question: why not a bit of both? Here's a useful piece of advice from a former boss:

> People will tell you not to take business personally. But they are wrong. The majority of your waking adult life will be spent at work. Not with your family. Not with your friends. If you don't take your business personally, then each day you come into work you will die a little. You must bring yourself into work.

Art and science aren't incompatible, in the same way that business and pleasure aren't incompatible. Nor are they substitutable. They complement one another. It would be absurd to argue that management science doesn't have a valuable role to play in making businesses more efficient. But it is equally absurd to deny that there is an art to making businesses great. Businesses rely for their success on people and personality as much as they do on protocol and process. This is why we describe business as a "hard art".

The five hallmarks of beautiful business

Stendhal described beauty as "La promesse de Bonheur" – the promise of happiness. This is at the heart of our enlarged concept of business, which embraces unmeasurables like creativity, initiative, passion and trust.

Businesses are created by people, for the purpose of making people happy. This people-centric approach presents us with an opportunity to draw from a much deeper well of inspiration, ideas and insight. Alexander Nehamas, in his study[5] exploring Stendhal's theme, says that to find something beautiful is to want to make it part of your life. Thinking about business – what is it that makes us want business to be part of our lives? Not just a single facet, but a number of different characteristics, subjective as well as factual.

This arms us with a set of (at least) five qualities that help us to challenge conventional wisdom: integrity, curiosity, craft, elegance and prosperity. Each of these "Hallmarks" encompasses our interpretation of the ingredients that make up beautiful business; not a measurement, but rather a framework for a different discussion about business in the world today.

Integrity

Beautiful businesses have a clear sense of purpose. A noble, unwavering belief that translates into firm principles for how to succeed. This is where a company's soul resides. This is what makes a business authentic, and being open and honest should be a precondition for business. Businesses are defined as much by their sacrifices as by their actions.

We look at the importance of integrity, purpose and belief in driving forward a business and introduce four businesses that demonstrate how integrity creates direction and desire.

Curiosity

A firm set of principles is essential to creating authenticity and setting standards within a business. But standards shouldn't mean standardisation. The ideals around which a business is built should not act as a straitjacket, stifling innovation and progress; they should instead act as a springboard for creativity. If necessity is the mother of invention, then curiosity is its father.

Beautiful businesses do not stand still. They are restless. They are brave. They are intrepid. They create constant surprise because they look at the world with originality and optimism. We discuss the importance of curiosity, bravery and optimism in the world of business. When does it pay to be daring? How do established businesses stay fresh? We introduce four businesses that demonstrate how curiosity influences productivity and profitability.

Elegance

Elegance in business is not a simple matter of aesthetics. It is a matter of problem-solving. A demonstration of empathy towards your audiences. It enables businesses to defy time and extend their influence over centuries.

Beautiful businesses are pleasurably simple. They find intelligent ways of doing things. They understand that persuasive presentation is a prerequisite for performance. Style and sophistication are tools for success. We demonstrate how this results in visibly better businesses, exploring how this can improve the ways that businesses interact with people. We introduce four businesses that demonstrate how the idea of elegance translates into leadership.

Craft

Technology has created countless opportunities for businesses to streamline, outsource and economise. The definition of what is possible is forever shifting. However, the definition of what is desirable is not so fluid, because people don't change as much as technology does. We like to see evidence of a human hand in the products we buy and the services we experience, a tangible demonstration of care that in turn makes the rest of us care about what a business does.

Beautiful businesses apply consideration to every last detail, no matter how small. A human hand guides. Beauty doesn't happen without devotion. We explore the relevance of craft to business, the obsession with the quality of the whole experience, and introduce four businesses that demonstrate a commitment to craft and attention to detail.

Prosperity

We all know that there's no point being in business if you're not going to make money. Profit is imperative in the short-term for survival and in the long-term for innovation and growth. Profit aids bold decision-making. But the decisions we make as businesspeople have implications beyond the P&L and Balance Sheet. They affect employees and their families and friends. They affect surrounding communities and businesses. They affect the environment. They influence us culturally, subjecting us to language, images, products and services that have a profound effect on how we think, feel and behave. It seems absurd to suggest that none of these considerations should factor into our definition of a successful business.

Short-term evaluation of profit is necessary but not sufficient. John Maynard Keynes famously said that "In the long run, we are all dead." But we are a long time alive. Businesses sustain our quality of life, so it is in our interests to ensure that our approach to business is sustainable in itself. It isn't in anybody's interests to sacrifice long-term prosperity for short-term profit (particularly for those of us who pay into a pension fund). Nor is it the case that long-term value-creation necessarily comes at the expense of near-term profitability. Profit is difficult to generate without influence. And influence is created through investment in people, community, culture and — increasingly — the environment. This is the intangible currency in which business success is most meaningfully measured. This is what we commonly understand as "goodwill". It accounts for over two-thirds of the value of the S&P 500.[6] It is critical to a business' health.

Beautiful businesses have a meaningful concept of value creation. They make a positive contribution to their owners, employees, customers, suppliers, society and the environment. People and the planet matter as much as profit. Businesses are capable of producing not just wealth, but a lasting heritage their legacy is not just financial success, but a strong business capable of long life and development. We look at four businesses that demonstrate how adopting a broader definition of value results in greater success and influence.

This book is a celebration of the businesses that have inspired us with their ability to create prosperity through the application of integrity, curiosity, craft and elegance. It is also a celebration of those unmeasurable drivers of success. Few of the themes we discuss lend themselves to quantification, but they are difficult to argue against as desirable and valuable aspects of business. We have purposefully chosen businesses of all shapes and sizes. Beauty is not the exclusive preserve of niche start-ups teamed by idealists. The bigger the company, the greater its ability to create prosperity.

We have also chosen businesses from all over the world because we believe the principles and themes this book covers transcend cultural differences. Concepts such as integrity, curiosity, elegance, craft and prosperity are universal. Beauty in business is at its heart a story about people and our capacity to care and to work together. We make no claim to be definitive or exhaustive in their selection. This isn't a "top 20 most beautiful businesses" league table. Our aim is to celebrate those qualities that make business a worthwhile and rewarding pursuit. The rest of this book is a journey through these qualities of beauty in business.

Summary map

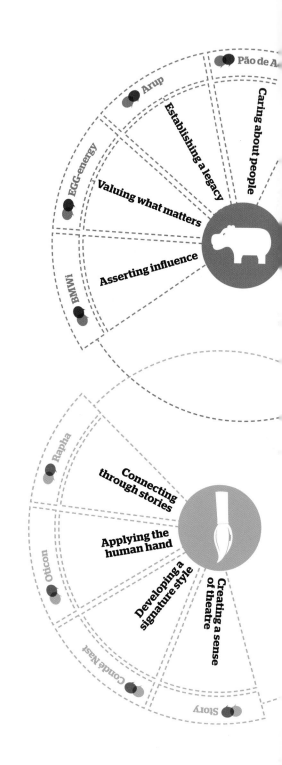

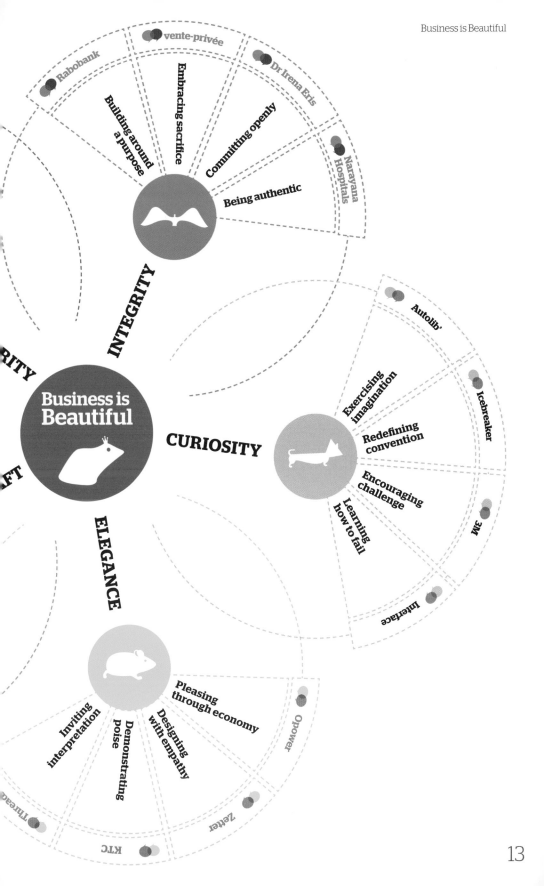

Business is Beautiful

INTEGRITY
- Building around a purpose
- Embracing sacrifice
- Committing openly
- Being authentic

Rabobank
vente-privée
Dr Irena Eris
Narayana Hospitals

CURIOSITY
- Exercising imagination
- Redefining convention
- Encouraging challenge
- Learning how to fail

Autolib'
Icebreaker
3M
Interface

ELEGANCE
- Pleasing through economy
- Designing with empathy
- Demonstrating poise
- Inviting interpretation

OPower
Zetter
KTC
Threadless

Integrity

Building around a purpose
Embracing sacrifice
Being authentic
Committing openly

Building around a purpose

If purpose is the quality of being determined to achieve something, and the reason for which something exists, what is the purpose of business?

You could say that the purpose of a business is ostensibly to generate profit. But to what end? A substantial portion of the profit a business makes is typically reinvested to safeguard future profit, which will in turn be reinvested. Framed this way, it's difficult to make business sound like a worthwhile pursuit. There is no sense of progress here. Peter Drucker suggested that while profit is a measure of the validity of a business, "it is not the explanation, cause, or rationale of business and business decisions".[7]

W.L. Gore & Associates (Gore) is probably best known as the creator of Gore-Tex fabric. The company was co-founded in 1958 by Wilbert "Bill" Lee Gore, together with his wife, Vieve. They started the company with a clear purpose in mind:

"To make money and have fun doing so."

And they succeeded. From its humble beginnings in the Gores' Newark basement, the company is now one of the 200 largest privately held businesses in the US, with annual revenues of US$3 billion and 9,500 employees. In 2012, for the fifteenth consecutive year, Gore was included in Fortune's annual list of the US "100 Best Companies to Work For", as well as featuring in equivalent lists in the UK, Germany, Italy, France and Sweden. Gore also features in the FastCompany 50 most innovative companies. What's interesting is how Gore has achieved such phenomenal growth without sacrificing the company's culture: they are frequently described by journalists as "a big company that behaves like a start-up". Bill Gore founded the company on an unwavering set of guiding principles that are still used today to unite the organisation:

> **Freedom:** The company believes that associates (employees) will exceed expectations when given the freedom to do so; action is prized; ideas are encouraged; and making mistakes is viewed as part of the creative process.
> **Fairness:** Everyone at Gore sincerely tries to be fair with each other, suppliers, customers, and anyone else with whom they do business.
> **Commitment:** Tasks are not assigned; rather, each person makes his own commitments and keeps them.
> **Waterline:** Everyone at Gore consults with other associates before taking actions that might be "below the waterline" – causing serious damage to the company.

Respect, responsibility and trust are central aspects of Gore's "lattice" approach to "un-management". Eschewing a traditional pyramidal management structure, Bill Gore created a flat organisational structure where everyone shares the title of "associate". Associates elect to follow leaders rather than having bosses assigned to them. Associate contribution reviews are based on a peer-level rating system. The entire business is run according to voluntary commitment. For many of us, this is difficult to reconcile with an ambitious, growing and profitable organisation. When Bill Gore was confronted with the incompatibility between the competing goals of a "human business" and a "profitable business", he responded in the following way:

> That's because there's something wrong with your education, sir. Actually, making money is a creative activity. It means people are applauding you for making a good contribution. In fact, it gives us the freedom to be what we are.

Gore's success is a vivid demonstration of the potential rewards that can accompany a re-humanisation of business, built on foundations of trust and respect. It is evidence that you don't have to be "mean" to be "lean". Traditional pyramid structures are built on the assumption that without sufficient supervision from above, employees will misbehave or lack direction. In economic terms, this is known as the "principal-agent problem" and describes the difficulty in motivating one party (the agent) to act on behalf of another party (the principal). Economists like to solve this problem with financial incentives that encourage "good" behaviour. This is because economists have traditionally seen humans as self-interested individuals, rather than as well-intentioned, rounded individuals who care about friendship, ethics and community. Fortunately, people are more complex and interesting than economists would have us believe. We are motivated by far more than just money, and there's plenty of evidence to demonstrate

We are motivated by far more than just money and there's plenty of evidence to demonstrate that financial incentives can be counter-productive.

that financial incentives can be counter-productive in situations where we tend to rely on people's goodwill for their good behaviour. The most famous example of this is an experiment conducted by Uri Gneezy and Aldo Rustichini in 2000[8], in which an Israeli day care centre began charging parents a small fine for being late in picking up their children. Rather than encouraging greater compliance, the system of fines actually resulted in an increase in the number of late pick-ups. Even after the system was removed, the parents who had faced the fines were more likely to be late in picking up their children than parents who had never been involved in the system. The argument goes that financial incentives "crowd out" our sense of moral responsibility to behave well. By introducing a penalty system, the day care centre signalled to parents that it lacked faith in them to act as responsible adults. Removing the penalty wasn't sufficient to restore this faith.

People-centric businesses understand that faith in people can be a powerful motivator. Faith on the part of the employer confers freedom on employees, which requires greater individual responsibility. The freedom Gore permits its employees is built on a firm belief in the individual:

> If you trust individuals and believe in them, they will be motivated to do what's right for the company.

In Gore's case, this has turned out to be a self-fulfilling prophecy. The reverse is also true: if you do not demonstrate faith in your employees, they are likely to under-perform. In homage to George Bernard Shaw's play, J. Sterling Livingston labelled this the "Pygmalion Effect". *Pygmalion* explores the idea that the expectations we place on other people influence how they behave. As the play's lead character, Eliza Doolittle, explains to Colonel Pickering:

> You see, really and truly, apart from the things anyone can pick up (the dressing and the proper way of speaking, and so on), the difference between a lady and a flower girl is not how she behaves but how she's treated. I shall always be a flower girl to Professor Higgins because he always treats me as a flower girl and always will; but I know I can be a lady to you because you always treat me as a lady and always will.

The expectations we have of the people we work with influence their performance: higher expectations promote confidence and motivate better performance; lower expectations can be communicated through countless signals – conscious and unconscious – that are demotivating and ultimately counter-productive. At the root of Gore's success is a combination of respect and reinforcing optimism. The company was established with a clear purpose and sustained through a simple set of principles. The beauty of Gore's business is that these beliefs have remained intact,

A clear statement of ambition inspires us to invest in, buy from and work for a business.

unchanged and relevant for over fifty years. It is in the soul of companies like W.L. Gore & Associates that integrity lies.

Many of the businesses we work with appreciate the importance of defining their purpose. They are in search of a compelling argument in favour of their continued existence: a reason for potential investors, employees and customers to engage with them. Profit maximisation doesn't cut the mustard. This comes across as unimaginative and undifferentiating. It is taken as a given that any business should aim to achieve profitability. The onus is on companies to describe exactly how and why they intend to create profit. A clear statement of ambition inspires us to invest in, buy from and work for a business. It should be clear how this ambition would result in profit, but the ambition itself cannot be defined in terms of profitability without falling into the trap of banality and circularity.

Consider the following statements of ambition, both of which are reproduced from the websites of two well-known banks:

Bank A:
Our company was built with hard work over 200 years. We would like to create a company that all can be proud of, and we are confident that, working together, we will build the best financial services company in the world.

Bank B:
Our banking practices always take a responsible approach to the development of wealth and prosperity. We respect the environment and the differing cultures and customs of the countries we operate in and we understand that maintaining our solvency and liquidity is a prerequisite for continuity.

Which of these banks would you prefer to invest in? Which would you prefer to work for? Which would you rather give your custom to? Bank B is Rabobank, which is regarded as one of the world's strongest banks.

There are striking differences between the ambitions articulated above: one is confident, empathetic and communicates specific commitments; the other is haughty and deliberately ambiguous. Confidence begets confidence. We are attracted to businesses that provide a vivid description of the world they intend to create. Amazon wants "to build a place where people can come to find and discover anything they might want to buy online". Method wants to make products that are "safe for every surface, especially earth's". Patagonia aims to "build the best product, cause no unnecessary harm, use business to inspire and implement solutions to the environmental crisis".

These are bold and brave statements to make. Expressed in such terms, success will be extremely difficult – potentially impossible – to achieve. But this is precisely what makes these businesses so fascinating. Big companies are built on big ideas. The clarity of these ambitions creates belief.

Another remarkable aspect of Rabobank's ambition is that it explicitly positions profit as a means and not an end in itself. This seems odd for a bank. We expect bankers to be driven solely by profit, not simply to "understand that maintaining solvency and liquidity is a prerequisite for continuity". But given the current perception and reputation of banking, integrity should surely be a goal, and re-establishing trust is a must for the future.

If you ask someone why they teach, you'd be pretty shocked if they were to answer "Because it pays well". It's highly likely that it doesn't. Teaching is a vocation. We expect teachers to be motivated by a desire to educate future generations, just as we expect doctors to be motivated by a desire to make people better. These motives matter to us. How many people would feel comfortable seeking treatment at a hospital that aims to maximise shareholder value?

We speak of teachers, doctors, counsellors and firemen "answering a calling". We expect that they are driven by a sense of purpose to choose their profession. So why not expect the same of people in business? Profit is necessary for businesses in the same way that a decent wage is necessary for employees. Businesses that are serious about attracting the best talent do not simply offer the highest incentives. They offer a sense of purpose that motivates great people to believe their talents will be meaningfully employed.

A global survey by research agency BlessingWhite in 2011[9] demonstrated how engaged employees "stay for what they give", while disengaged employees "stay for what they get". In other words, financial incentives may help a business to retain people, but they don't work so well in terms of motivating them to do a good job. We can't rely on profit to motivate people to create great work; their motivation has to come from elsewhere.

There's a paradox at work here. Shareholder value relies upon a significant and stable stream of future profit. This profit in turn relies upon a business' ability to inspire loyalty among its customers and employees. But organisations that obsess over shareholder value or profit necessarily do so at the expense of customer intimacy, product quality and employee commitment, which erodes customer and employee loyalty, which restricts value-creation. The surest way to create a stable, profitable business isn't to focus on profit at all, but to focus instead on its underlying drivers.

We analysed the 50 largest companies in the S&P 500 and split them into two groups. The first group explicitly mention value-creation in their statements of ambition. This group achieved an average Price-to-Book Ratio of 2.8*. The second group of companies – including Apple, Google, IBM and Amazon.com – do not explicitly mention financial objectives in their statements of ambition, yet achieved a Price-to-Book Ratio of 4.6 – substantially higher than the financially driven group. This chimes with Peter Drucker's notion that profitability is a measure of validity, not a source of motivation in business. A clearly defined purpose is not a luxury. It's central to a business that intends to be successful in the long-term.

S&P top 50 Companies
(July 2012)

Price to book ratio

5.0

2.5

2.8

4.6

Purpose-driven companies

Profit-chasing companies

*Analysis conducted 30 July 2012

Rabobank
Stability, continuity and solidity

In many respects Rabobank appears to be the quintessence of a traditional bank.
It can trace its roots back to the mid-Nineteenth Century, when Friedrich Wilhelm Raiffeisen created the first farmer's bank in Germany.

Photograph by Alexander van Berge for Rabobank Netherlands

The bank prides itself on its reliability. Rabobank was number 10 in Global Finance's 2012 ranking of the World's Safest Banks' and was ranked at number 26 in The Banker's list of 'The Top 1000 World Banks', ahead of France's Societe Generale and Spain's BBVA.

But Rabobank's folksy roots belie a radical and distinctive organisation. In the traditional banking model, local branches tend to be owned by a central organisation. In Rabobank's case, however, the opposite is true: the network of local Rabobanks is the mother of the central organisation. Rabobank doesn't have a 'head office' so much as a 'support office'. Vincent Lokin is Rabobank's Head of Cooperative and Governance. His role is to make sure that this cooperative approach to banking works. It's an approach based on common sense, where decisions are made by people. *"I think it is important to understand our history in order to understand our reason of being. We were not founded by people who had money and wanted to make more money. We were founded by people with limited access to money who decided to organise*

Building around a purpose | Rabobank

themselves to achieve more. And the single purpose of this cooperative was to serve its members and its clients. That's all. Nothing more. But in order to achieve this you need to generate order. To create a sustainable organisation. To comply with the rules of the larger system. Making money is an important aspect, because in the interests of our clients and of the bank we need stability, continuity and solidity. In order to maintain that we need to make profit. Profit is a means through which to serve our clients. It is not a goal to pursue for its own end, or for our shareholders, which is an important difference compared with listed banks."

Lokin is joined in our conversation by Bouke de Vries, Rabobank's Head of Financial Sector Research. His team analyses the financial sector, following regulatory changes and competitive activity in retail banking. He is ideally placed to talk about Rabobank's structure and position in the Dutch financial sector.

"In the present situation of financial turmoil and markets, the robust capital position of the Rabobank and conservative risk management are important. This builds trust. The fact that we are a cooperative means that we are closely positioned towards customers. This is especially relevant today, as the banking sector is facing a lack of trust. I believe we should invite debate with our members and customers about important questions such as: what went wrong during the credit crisis? How can we rethink banking? And what are the main functions of a bank?"

Debate is a recurring theme in our conversation. According to de Vries, "The main point of the cooperative model is that it is democratic and a key aspect of this is that you are willing to be held accountable. "The executive board has the authority to set the strategy but they have to ask for approval for the strategy from the (now) 138 local

member banks. They send delegates to the Central Delegates Assembly, which is our 'parliament'. As an example, if the local member banks say with good reason that they would like to have the strategy changed, then the strategy will be changed. At the local level, in turn, Rabobank has around 1.9 million members. It is harder to organise debate with millions of members than with 138 member banks, so we've developed other instruments to help to do this, like the Advisory Council, where entrepreneurs and citizens have opportunities to engage with the bank."

It's hard to deny the work that has gone into Rabobank's cooperative structure is impressive. Democracy and debate are desirable in theory but all too often lead to inefficiency, inflexibility and an inability to set clear strategy in practice. This is acknowledged by Lokin and de Vries. "Decisions may take longer. However, when they have to be enacted, they also have a broader support." Lokin adds: "Structure alone isn't enough. A structure is just a set of pipelines through which information travels. If the information runs freely then the cooperative model can work. That's an important part of my role. You cannot be the head of a cooperative. All you can do is act as a catalyst for the system."

De Vries agrees: "This is about structure and culture. Our bottom-up structure facilitates this kind of democratic debate, but it is the culture and the people that make the difference. We enable a lot of autonomy at a low level to make decisions that are in the best interest of the customers. So the local banks and the advisors that face the customers have a lot of authority to make decisions and our organisation should support these local banks to be as effective as possible."

"The main role of any bank is to finance the real economy. This is also the case for

Building around a purpose | Rabobank

Photograph by Alexander van Berge for Rabobank Netherlands

cooperative banks. The main difference is that members control cooperatives and that cooperatives have a decentralised form of organisation. Cooperative banks are historically oriented to do business locally and this is still very much the case. It's an economic model with socially beneficial outcomes. Each of the members should see their goals being accomplished by the cooperative. It is an economic model based on a common purpose and the socially beneficial outcome is that you contribute to local development because you are financing the real economy at a local level. You provide access to finance. You provide access for citizens to financial products. This sounds very logical in theory but it isn't practiced in the developed world today. During the credit crisis we saw a rift emerge between customers and providers of financial services. We are able to go to these customers and say 'we believe in you as an entrepreneur'."

This idea of providing finance to entrepreneurs and helping to kick-start the real economy is extremely alluring in the context of a financial crisis. After all, entrepreneurs make up the bulk of our economies. And Vincent Lokin points out that Rabobank has more to offer than just financial support:

"We want to add value to the society we are in. Not just with money but with our network, our knowledge and our people. We are in a position to make a difference, by supporting the global food system and by making it possible that the 9 billion people living on the planet in 2050 can eat. A lot of the large parties in food and agriculture are our clients but in order to feed 9 billion people, it will be necessary to introduce more small farmers to the system. The way to do it is to encourage them to work together as a cooperative, to develop them and to connect them to the food system. We think we can teach them

to work together. It requires knowledge more than money.
"We support groups of people in rural areas who could be assisted to set up a cooperative. This is not always about financial support, but a matter of technical assistance. After 3-7 years, such groups are capable of developing into a saving cooperative able to lend money to its members and to use its profits to make the system stronger. We tell them we have been doing this for 114 years. It is great for us to see that these groups become independent from us within a few years.

"As a large bank in the food and agriculture industry we have direct access to large traders, processors and distributors of food. And we also finance local producer cooperatives, so we can contribute to the improvement of opportunities for developing countries and producer cooperatives by giving them access to these global food supply chains, by linking them to our other customers – the larger companies."

This sounds like a tremendously satisfying situation: Rabobank bringing together a network of smallholders, entrepreneurs and global food giants to support an increasingly hungry planet. But our interviewees don't paint an entirely rosy picture. Not all of the entrepreneurs Rabobank works with are destined to succeed. And not even Rabobank can satisfy all of its customers all of the time. As Vincent Lokin explains to us, customer satisfaction is taken extremely seriously at Rabobank, but it isn't the most important measure of success for a cooperative that tries to do the right thing:
"Our customer satisfaction research shows that customers are being heard. But this situation is complex because sometimes our customers are dissatisfied when we don't sell them what they want. If we measure their satisfaction [at that time] it

probably isn't the best, but we hope that if we go back a year later, they realise why we did what we did. We don't put the client first. We put the client's interests first.

"Our credit losses on mortgage loans and the number of arrears, which are already historically very low in the Netherlands, are significantly lower than average. We think this is one of the effects of being a cooperative bank, of being interested in your clients and having the guts to say no to your clients, even if you know they won't like you at the end of the meeting. Thanks to our conservative risk policy, we are in a good position to well withstand the current less favourable circumstances in the Dutch housing market. We are an important pillar in the system, therefore it is in our own, as well as the client's, interest that we take a prudent approach in our lending activities."

Maintaining such a level of integrity is a huge responsibility to take on. Vincent Lokin is clear on one final point: Rabobank's own integrity relies on the extent to which it takes its own values seriously. This means those values must be constantly explained and questioned.

'I think it is good to revisit our core values, not just to assume they persist because they are perfect. I have always tried to understand them. It can sometimes mean we don't sell a product. For example, we are in the middle of an interesting discussion about how we can measure the performance of our employees, because the one that sells the most mortgages is not likely to be the person that always works in the best interests of our clients. So how can we resolve supporting our clients' interests with our commercial requirement to make enough money to keep the system going?

It is a tension and challenge. But it is our intention to keep discussing this. The moment we stop the discussion we are lost."

Embracing sacrifice

Articulating a purpose isn't enough. Unless you are prepared to sacrifice potentially lucrative sources of business to achieve your vision, it's extremely easy for audiences to grow cynical about bold statements of ambition. This is about what you choose not to do, making tough decisions to remain who you are, true to your central purpose and values.

Sacrifice isn't a popular term in the context of business. We aren't talking about the kind of sacrifice that results in missing your children's birthdays or divorcing your spouse. We have no interest in celebrating martyrdom in business. The type of sacrifice we're interested in is a corollary of strategic focus. Businesses can be defined by the actions and opportunities they avoid in the single-minded pursuit of their long-term ambition. It's easy to talk about the importance of focus; it's much more difficult to embrace the virtue of sacrifice.

One of our favourite rules of thumb is the 80-20 rule, which broadly states that 80% of outcomes are determined by 20% of inputs. This rule can be usefully applied to a number of situations, for example:

> 80% of your profit comes from 20% of your product range
> 80% of your sales come from 20% of your customers.

The implication is clear: your time is more profitably spent focusing on the 20% of inputs that will have a bigger impact on the success of your business. We've worked with lots of organisations to help them rationalise their product ranges, to identify profitable customer segments and to allocate investment across business units based on their ability to create incremental growth. These decisions are always based on more specific data than the 80-20 rule, but it's surprising how frequently more detailed calculations result in the same outcome. It's also surprising how reluctant many people are to make the tough decisions that the 80-20 rule implies.

Let's take customer segmentation as an example. In theory, this is a relatively straightforward affair. You work out which audiences are most vital to the success of your organisation. You understand what makes them tick. Then you align your products and services to reflect this understanding. Segmenting customers can be immensely fun... Identifying groups of people with differing motivations... Christening them with evocative names... Picking the segments most aligned with your business' goals... This is quantitative analysis at its sexiest and most alluring. But there is a murky side to the 80-20 rule. It feels constructive to focus on the 20% of customers who will make the biggest difference to your business. But it's not so much fun to contemplate the 80% of people that you will have to de prioritise in order to achieve this focus.

It seems horribly mean to say we're going to turn our backs on 80% of the people we could be dealing with. Disregarding potentially relevant audiences feels shameful and, more importantly, it seems limiting from a commercial perspective. Why would you deliberately choose to fish in a smaller pond? Many business leaders want to eat their cake and have it. They wish they could enjoy the benefits of a targeted approach without sacrificing less valuable relationships. But unless you have unlimited time and resources, it simply isn't possible to focus equally on every potential customer segment. The act of prioritising one group of people necessarily involves de-prioritising everybody else. Businesses that try to please everybody equally end up pleasing nobody in particular. So prioritisation is necessary.

To take a real-world example, let's look at Patagonia, which aims to "build the best product, cause no unnecessary harm, use business to inspire and implement solutions to the environmental crisis". Being eco-friendly turns out not to be very wallet-friendly: a single pair of men's underpants costs US$25. Patagonia can't achieve its purpose if it doesn't survive as a profitable business, which means it needs to find people who are willing to invest nearly US$200 just to keep themselves in clean underpants for a week. This is why Patagonia's store locations read like a list of the world's most affluent neighbourhoods: SoHo in New York, Santa Monica in California, Covent Garden in London, Mejiro in Tokyo, Chapel Street in Melbourne.

The Patagonia business model relies on maintaining loyal, lasting relationships with a small group of environmentally enlightened, financially comfortable citizens. Speaking at a conference in 2006, executives from Patagonia estimated that 64% of customers are one-time purchasers who do not buy again. Of the remaining 36%, a smaller group – cutely referred to as "cheerleaders" – contribute disproportionately to revenue, as well as driving advocacy. It seems the 80-20 rule also applies in Patagonia's case (give or take).[10] The company's founder, Yves Chouinard, described his approach to segmentation and sacrifice in beautifully succinct terms: "If you're not pissing off 50% of the people, you're not trying hard enough."[11]

There is a flipside to the observation that being nonspecific in an attempt to appeal to everybody usually results in appealing to nobody: targeting a specific audience gives everybody else something distinct to identify with. Hopefully the audience you are seeking to attract will identify with your business in the way you intend. But this doesn't mean that the audiences you've chosen to de-prioritise will necessarily be turned off. Instead, they are likely to identify with your business in their own way. It's much more likely that this will happen if you give a person something specific to respond to – even if he or she isn't the audience you had in mind. You may not be at a point in your life when you're prepared to spend 25 dollars on a pair of ethically produced, ecologically sound Y-fronts, but they're out there if you want them.

Sacrifice may not be comfortable, but it is necessary if a business intends to achieve its long-term goals and keep its soul in the process. Howard Schultz returned to Starbucks in 2008, when the spirit of the business he had originally established in 1971 was seriously under threat. Amongst his long list of complaints of the wayward business was over-exposure of a uniform retail concept, the introduction of new coffee machines that hindered customers' views of the baristas at work, as well as coffee shops that no longer smelt of coffee because the beans were shipped and stored in sealed aluminium bags. Starbucks had become a business with a premium offer that no longer felt special, exciting or novel. In their 2005 "Encyclopedia of modern life", Steve Lowe and Alan McArthur summed up their disillusionment with the ubiquity of Starbucks' excessive and aggressive approach to brand growth:

> How utterly unimpressed with life's infinite possibilities would you have to be to go to Starbucks and read a book about Starbucks, by Starbucks, while having a Starbucks?[12]

This was a far cry from the company's stated mission: "to inspire and nurture the human spirit — one person, one cup and one neighbourhood at a time." Schultz's response must have seemed brutal for those involved: in his first year back at the helm, Starbucks closed 600 stores and cut 6,700 jobs.[13] In the last quarter of the same year, Starbucks reported a 97% decline in profit. But there's a happy ending. According to its 2011 Annual Report, Starbucks revenues, income and margin have increased steadily in each year since 2009. Reflecting on his strategy in an interview with SUCCESS in March 2012, Howard Schultz outlined the importance of the company's purpose in turning around the business:

> For Starbucks, the key to our success has always been finding a balance between profitability and social conscience. It is easy to abandon ideals when a ship is sinking and just row. But our values steadied us when our stock, our reputation and our performance were all at their lowest points. Our belief in our purpose as a company — in the knowledge that how we do business matters to customers as well as shareholders — gave us the courage and will to turn the ship around. Values are not luxuries for prosperous times. They are necessities in all times.

vente-privee:
Strategic inconvenience

Jacques-Antoine Granjon has been in business for 28 years, and in 2001 launched vente-privee, an online company that organises exclusive online flash sales for high quality brands seeking to "destock" last season's products.

Courtesy of vente-privee

Granjon is not a typical businessman. He sports a flowing mane of chestnut hair that reaches far beyond his shoulders. He prefers boots to brogues. And he's more likely to be seen in a necklace than a tie. Similarly, vente-privee is not a typical business: 'sacrifice' and 'success' go hand-in-hand. At the heart of vente-privee is a paradox: how can you sell destocked luxury items at a discount without cheapening the brands involved?

Granjon's solution to this paradox is to establish a sense of worth by sacrificing one of the key benefits of the Internet: its ability to democratise access to products, services and information. Often referred to as 'strategic inconvenience', the limited information available to visitors to the

vente-privee website that are not yet registered helps maintain an element of value and preciousness for the brands it sells and creates a feeling of discovery and intrigue for customers. *"All that was invented on vente-privee wasn't done thinking about the customer, but thinking about the brand. A large stock of unsold items can destroy the image if they're sold in any old way. These unsold items must be channelled and that's the essence of my business."*

"Everyone thinks vente-privee is a private club as we want to add value to our members, the brands and the community. What is true is that it's a club to prevent search engines from coming to my site to look for brand prices and put them on Google, which would damage the image of

Embracing sacrifice | vente-privee

Photograph by Clément Schneider, courtesy of vente-privee

the brands. It's a club because the sales event is hidden. It can't be exposed on the outside in order to protect the brands."

At the heart of Granjon's concept of 'strategic inconvenience' is an insight into how desire is created. We tend to value things more when we have to work to find them. It might be easier to find cheap luxury items through Google, but where's the fun in that? Particularly when it comes to luxury items, we want to be teased. We want to be tempted. *"Amazon, the e-commerce giant, currently represents need: you need something, anything, and you go to Amazon. And in ten years, it will be a question of answering even greater needs, from the low end to the high end. I plan to be the opposite of Amazon. I'm going to create desire and create desirable events. To succeed on the Internet, two things are necessary and Amazon is based on them: a very large range of products and an extremely high level of customer service.*

I have a very large range of products and I have a high-level of service for customers and brands. vente-privee is desire, Amazon is need."

This is not a niche strategy. vente-priveé's sales are €1.3 billion, of which France accounts for 80%. There's still plenty of room to grow. But Granjon isn't in a hurry. The story of vente-privee is a long one and is as much a personal tale as a story about business.

"It's the story of a guy who lives in France and wants to be independent. He doesn't want to work in a 'structure' because he doesn't fit into one and doesn't want to take orders. He doesn't know how to do everything, but he does like to surround himself with competent people. Above all, vente-privee is an adventure involving people. Julien Sorbac was my partner from the beginning, Mickael Benabou joined us four years later and my brother-in-law

Xavier Court fifteen years ago. Even my wife Eleonore has been working with us since 1994. I have always thought of this company as a human adventure, with shared enjoyment, freedom and independence, with an economic goal at the start."

It becomes clear in our discussion that the enjoyment of freedom and independence comes at a price. Adopting a policy of 'strategic inconvenience' requires a tremendous amount of tenacity. vente-priveé's success hasn't gone unnoticed over the years. Potential competitors have been queuing up to knock the business off its perch, typically with the same idea: 'if vente-privee has managed to build a successful business by making life inconvenient for people, just imagine how much opportunity exists for a similar business that offers convenience instead'.

"The copiers started to show up in 2007, they observed what we were doing and found it rather easy. There were 500 copiers throughout the world in the space of two years. They took two years to create their business and arrived on the market in 2009. Some people have a short-term vision and pull out in front, but those with a long-term vision are the final winners. You need to be a frustrated pessimist. A businessman who's too optimistic can be naïve. But naïvety doesn't belong in a company because, to my way of thinking, only the paranoid survive. I am always paranoid and on the defensive. I have a motto, the Latin saying: "Capitolium saxo proxima" (A fall from grace can come quickly). You can be on the pinnacle like a powerful senator and then be hurled to a shameful death... from the very same place."

Granjon's formula for avoiding such a tragic and dramatic fall from grace is a characteristic combination of simplicity and contrariness in an industry so frequently accused of frivolity and faddishness.

"What is important is why we do things. Success is achieved through the realisation that you should never forget what is essential and why you are doing something. I am not someone who would sell his company because I think we can still do much better. In the 2000s I asked myself: how can I ensure the long-term survival of my business? I came up with wrong tracks and dead ends. It's the same with life; it's a labyrinth. All the changes in my company are tied to a constant search for integrity, a search to find how to do as well as possible in my business. The success of vente-privee is based on constancy."

Being authentic

The qualities of being upfront about what you do, straightforward in your dealings with your customers and employees, and sincere in your beliefs are essential foundations for the long-term health and growth of business. Honesty should be a prerequisite for being in business. Nobody wants to deal with a company that lies or cheats. Or do they? There are a staggering number of articles and books that champion the merits of Machiavellian business practices. For example, in 2011, Forbes published an article titled "5 Machiavellian Business Lessons From Billionaire Aliko Dangote".[14] Dangote is a self-made Nigerian billionaire; Africa's richest man, worth an estimated $14 billion, which Forbes implies is the result of a "cynical, eccentric, tactical, and manipulative" approach to doing business. Machiavelli's knack for dispensing advice in neat soundbites has made his political philosophy tempting fodder for business literature:

> 'A prince never lacks legitimate reasons to break his promise.'
> 'A wise ruler ought never to keep faith when by doing so it would be against his interests.'
> 'Before all else, be armed.'
> 'It is better to be feared than loved, if you cannot be both.'
> 'Men are so simple and so much inclined to obey immediate needs that a deceiver will never lack victims for his deceptions.'

One of the most popular lessons in Machiavellian business practice is the need to be a great "simulator" and "dissimulator". Leadership, it seems, requires a level of moral flexibility that is beyond the majority of mere mortals. A Machiavellian business leader cuts a very lonely figure and must employ a variety of underhand tactics to deceive his "simple victims" – more commonly referred to as colleagues – into helping him to achieve his ends.

Enthusiasm for a Machiavellian approach to business might be blunted by a brief look into his own success in life. While he served as a diplomat and led the Florentine militia, he also lost a war, lost his job, was accused of conspiracy, arrested, imprisoned and tortured, before being forced into early retirement. Not a nice way to end a career. Honesty, it seems, is a better policy, particularly when we consider how important trust is to the health of our economy and financial system. When we can't trust businesses to act honestly – to tell the truth and keep their promises – government, regulators and legislators step in to enforce good behaviour. In the US, the Sarbanes-Oxley Act was introduced in 2002 in direct response to a series of corporate scandals, including Tyco, Enron, and WorldCom. This legislation is intended to protect investors, but its costs are significant. In 2009 a group of academics from the Texas A&M University[15] sampled 1,428 firms in the US and found that Sarbanes-Oxley-related costs varied from around US$6 million for smaller firms to US$39 million for larger firms. In aggregate, the total cost of legislation across the businesses sampled exceeded US$19 billion. It seems evident that dishonesty costs us all a lot.

Honesty isn't just about avoiding bad behaviour. There are a handful of emergent companies that have demonstrated the potency of a more open and honest approach to business. Zappos seems to be the current darling of the business world and a favourite example of a more progressive, transparent approach to doing business. Most of the case studies we've read extol the importance of the company's values in creating a culture of success. Potential employees are screened against these values and new recruits are offered an incentive of US$2,000 to quit, as a test of their commitment to the company's ethos. But Zappos isn't alone in employing these methods, nor is it unique in promoting a culture that praises "weirdness" and "fun". What makes Zappos peculiar is the level of transparency with which the company communicates to employees, investors, customers and even suppliers.

You're not really being honest if you only choose to tell people happy truths and neglect to acknowledge that things don't always run smoothly.

This commitment is enshrined in the sixth of their ten values: Build Open And Honest Relationships With Communication. There are plenty of examples of how the business has followed through on this commitment: when the company shed 8% of its workforce in 2008, their Chief Executive sent a detailed email to employees to explain what was happening and why, as well as publishing his email on his blog for a wider audience to see; the company has also streamed internal meetings live over the internet, for everybody to see (including the competition). Even more significantly, this commitment to transparency has had fundamental implications for the company's approach to supply-chain management.

Zappos had originally employed a "drop ship" approach to inventory management, in which their suppliers would send shoes directly to their customers, minimising the amount of inventory Zappos needed to store. But efficiency came at a cost. Inventory feeds from suppliers were at best 95% accurate,[16] which meant that 5% of orders at any time were likely to be left unfulfilled, to the displeasure of Zappos' customer base. So the company switched to an inventory model and created an internal team to build a warehouse operation capable of transforming the customer experience from displeasure to delight.

This change of strategy had the potential to create an adversarial relationship with suppliers — it's easy to characterize them as the weak link in the supply chain. But instead of trying to squeeze its suppliers, Zappos gives them access to all of the information available to their own buyers. The idea is that if the average Zappos buyer works with fifty suppliers, then being transparent with those suppliers means you have fifty additional people helping you to run your business. Suppliers can see inventory levels, sales and profitability data. They can procure inventory on fast-selling items. They can make suggestions for Zappos buyers to approve. They can collaborate with Zappos' marketing team to plan marketing campaigns. Sharing information with suppliers has led to a shared responsibility for maintaining the integrity of the entire supply chain. Honesty doesn't just benefit the leaders of a business — it benefits everybody in the value chain.

There's something alluring about businesses that admit to their flaws.

A big problem with being honest is that no business is perfect. You're not really being honest if you only choose to tell people happy truths and neglect to acknowledge that things don't always run smoothly. The popularity of social media has made it extremely easy for people to find out for themselves when businesses fail to live up to the high expectations set by their communication. In 2011, a disgruntled customer posted a YouTube video of a FedEx driver "delivering" a computer monitor by carelessly tossing it over their front gate. In response, FedEx's Senior Vice President of the company's US operations posted a YouTube video in which he expressed his disappointment and embarrassment, as well as FedEx's determination to put things right with the customer in question. It seems the video is now used in employee training sessions.

Some companies prefer to pre-empt such crises by actively communicating their flaws. In 2010, Dominos Pizza famously launched a brutally honest US campaign, in which the company openly admitted its product was substandard and listed the measures they were taking to effect a turnaround. While it seemed like a tremendous risk at the time, the strategy paid off. In the first quarter of 2010, Domino's grew sales by 14.3% in the United States — the highest ever recorded jump in fast food history.[17]

There's something alluring about businesses that admit to their flaws. When it comes to people, we tend to read character into flaws. Perfection isn't a human trait, so we tend not to expect perfection from a human organisation. Being cynical about the culture of "spin" seems to have become embedded in business life. A relentless stream of good news is easily interpreted as a manipulation of the truth. It is also tedious and irritating. When we are well disposed to companies, we tend to see eccentricities rather than flaws. We see beauty in imperfection. Businesses, brands and products with cult followings are more frequently distinguished by their blemishes than their benefits. This is what lends them their authenticity.

Being authentic | Dr. Irena Eris

Dr. Irena Eris
Natural beauty

In Poland in 1983, Dr. Irena Eris had a vision for her business, and joined by her husband, Henryk Orfinger, she began the journey to the success it is today; founded on strong values and a belief in the quality of her products.

Courtesy of Dr. Irena Eris

Dr. Irena Eris says, *"When I look at my business over the last 30 years, at the beginning we didn't know very much, so we let our intuition guide us, and we managed. It was later that we wrote down the mission and vision, and then enriched them with our values and our management approach.*

"In 1983, there was no support for business from the authorities in Poland; private business was hardly allowed, only tolerated at a small, artisanal scale. The atmosphere around business wasn't good. We wanted to do something with passion, that would give us satisfaction, so we built our company step by step in a way that felt right to us."

The company started with one employee and one single product. Today there are over 800 employees, and the company produces twenty million units a year, with several hundred cosmetics products. The values around which they built the business still hold firm — quality, honesty, reliability, innovation, respect for people and a progressive approach to operations.

By 1989, the system in Poland had changed, it had joined the market economy, giving the business a chance to create a real brand. As the attitude and perception towards business changed,

Dr. Irena Eris became an icon in the local business world, demonstrating how a company could be developed. She told us, *"At last it was considered that business people, who take the risk of running their own company and providing people with jobs, work hard and pay taxes. It occurred to everyone that this should actually be supported because it boosts the economy."*

Dr. Irena Eris and her husband were ready to take the next step with their business – they bought land near Warsaw and built their own factory. They invested in up-to-date computer-controlled machines and hired more people to meet the demand created by their products.

At the same time, with the opening up of the market, Western products became available in Poland. Competition spurred Dr. Irena Eris to continue concentrating on quality, rather than cutting costs. *"We had this idée fixe, that we wanted everything to be done to the highest quality and this is what created our brand."*

Dr. Irena Eris's vision was extensive; being innovative was always at the heart of her strategy, not to follow the competition but to do something new. Sometimes, they even led the way, for example, by setting the holistic attitude towards beauty. *"It's more than producing just excellent quality beauty products, it's about giving possibility to our clients, so that they can take care of themselves holistically, be beautiful, feel better and help them achieve their personal goals."*

At the twenty-two Dr Irena Eris Skin Care Institutes there are qualified specialists and dermatologists using only Dr Irena Eris's products, the treatments are tailored to individual needs and preferences. They also opened the Spa Hotel in Krynica Zdrój in 1997. *"This hotel was experimental for us. Now we have two, with a third under construction in Polanica Zdrój. Each one has a Dr Irena Eris Skin Care Institute and its own Spa Centre with swimming pools, saunas and jacuzzis for the guests. They also offer a number of activities such as walking, cycling, tennis, horse riding and winter sports. There's something for everyone."*

When planning the opening of their second Dr Irena Eris SPA Hotel in Wzgórza Dylewskie, many hotel industry experts thought it wouldn't work. Irena Eris hired a global company to work with them on the project. *"We asked them to carry out some research, it was very extensive and expensive and their recommendation was that we shouldn't go ahead. But we believed in it, so we built it. And it turned out to be a success. Some time later, we were invited to the research company's anniversary and the CEO in his speech said about our project: 'We were wrong'. It was amazing. He didn't need to mention it at all. He did his job in the way that he thought was right, and that could have been it. But he said 'We were wrong'. I was very touched – it's very rare that people admit to their mistakes. I think that honesty is a very important quality when running a business, after all it's a responsibility. Taking responsibility for what you do. I have good intentions but if something comes out wrong – I say it. For me that's very important."*

The company also established its own Centre for Science and Research. Dr Irena Eris Cosmetic Laboratories is the only cosmetics manufacturer in Poland and one of the few in Europe and worldwide to carry out advanced research using in vitro, ex vivo and in vivo methods in their own Research Centre. Their scientists conduct research into skin physiology, in vitro research on external culture of skin cells, looking at how certain substances react with the skin's physiology, the best dosage and in which combination.

Being authentic | Dr. Irena Eris

Courtesy of Dr. Irena Eris

"Without this research we can never be sure of the final result when we create our products, and the purpose is, of course, to apply the results in products. Without this we can't know for certain if we're helping or damaging skin. We do the research because we want to be sure that those beauty products are exactly what we want them to be."

Research results are presented at international conferences and published in scientific journals, including major scientific periodicals including the ISI Master Journal List, a list of scientific journals created and updated by the *Institute for Scientific Information. "At first everyone was a bit surprised that we were at the congress because Poland was still perceived as it was when we were behind the* Iron Curtain. *After our lectures, our scientists were surrounded by groups of interested people, some of them wanted to collaborate with us, and we do this with a lot of institutions in Poland and abroad. For example, right now we are collaborating on a project devoted to biodegradable packaging. It makes us stronger. Maybe it's not very*

visible outside the company but it gives us a competitive advantage and credibility as an honest company. For us it's clear that we're honest and that when we say something, we need to have the research to back it up. We have to know that it's created by us from the very beginning. I sign the product, I take responsibility for it, and it's not just me, but all of our employees.

"I believe that my business is a creative activity. I would like every customer to be able to choose a product that's right for their skin because everyone needs something different. I've always respected our customers, I wanted to know what they wanted and I was always honest with them.

"I think it's crucial that a business creates a happy environment, with positive thinking and a belief that what we do is real, natural and honest. If there is any contradiction, a false message — whether at product or corporate level, sooner or later the customers or our staff will know about it. So I think that building a business in an optimistic, positive way and by being good to others is really valuable. I would like

everyone to take pleasure in coming to work, and then take these positive emotions back home to their family.

"When it comes to the way we work, there is of course innovation, responsibility, and respect – for people and for the environment. And of course we value our independence, we want our financial results to be good enough for us to have freedom of choice or action. It is important because we can speed up or delay our plans, which is not always that easy for listed companies, or for companies that have to be very careful about the numbers. Obviously, we look at the figures as well, but even if the numbers are not that good, we know that we are creating the future and we believe in it.

"Last year we received a letter from Comité Colbert, a French organisation created in 1954 by the founder of Guerlain. It's an association of the most luxurious brands, mostly French. The members include brands such as Guerlain, Chanel, Louis Vuitton, Hotel Ritz, Hermès, Cartier, Louvre, Sorbonne, Veuve Cliquot. It took six months to go through all the procedures, and finally after their formal board meeting we were accepted, and in June we received confirmation that we're members. It's very prestigious for us. The Association cares about business ethics and how the company works, what products it has, what are the chances for development and becoming an international company."

And here's a final word from Dr. Irena Eris on beautiful business, and what keeps her going: "It gives me joy. Not only me, but other people as well. There's a lot of talk about human capital and that's really the key for successful business, for development. Our business is not just about data, it's about intuition, imagination, respect and being honest. This is what's important, this is what makes us happy and what makes us want to go forward."

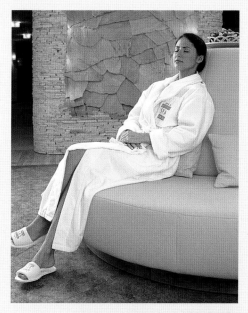

Courtesy of Dr. Irena Eris

Committing openly

When Carlos Ghosn took over as Chief Executive of Nissan in 1999, the company was in long-term decline and on the verge of bankruptcy. The 1990s had seen wave after wave of restructuring announcements, none of which had arrested the carmaker's sliding market share and profit. Despite this, shortly after his appointment, he made a dramatic pledge: he would resign if Nissan did not report an operating profit in the fiscal year ending March 2001. This claim looked all the more dramatic following the publication of a record operating loss of 684.36 billion yen in May 2000. After a remarkable twelve months, Carlos Ghosn presented financial results that not only made good on his promise to return the company to profitability – Nissan posted a record profit of 331.1 billion yen.[18]

In an interview with CNN in 2005, Mr. Ghosn attributed the success of the turnaround plan to three factors, all of which relate to the themes we've covered in this chapter:

> Number one is you have to establish with the people of the company a very simple vision about where we're going, what's the destination; where we're going has to be shared at all levels of the company.

> Number two, you have to have strategy; how do we get there, what are the action plans, and make sure they are deployed at every level of the company, everybody knows what is the contribution that is expected from him or from her for the company.

> Number three, people have to feel strong commitment coming from the top, personal commitment, team commitment coming from the top, we're here to revive the company and if you don't do it well we're out, we're out of here.

> At the end, results are going to cement everything, they're going to give you the credibility, they're going to make people feel safe about the company and wanting to join. Vision, strategy, commitment and results.[19]

Vision and strategy don't matter if you can't back them up with commitment. One of Nissan Europe's senior executives talked about the internal perceptions of the turnaround. He described the huge cultural shift that had underpinned the performance improvement. Prior to Mr. Ghosn's arrival, promises were easily made and easily broken. Former CEO Hanawa Yoshikazu labelled this a "culture of blame", in which it was common for different departments to work in isolation and then blame other departments for the failure that inevitably results from lack of cooperation. Ghosn describes this culture in his 2005 book, *Shift: Inside Nissan's Historic Revival*:

Nissan had gradually developed a culture in which the standard response to problems was "It's not me, it's someone else." If the company was in trouble, it was always the fault of other people. The sales department complained about product planning, thus effectively knocking the ball into the engineering department's court. Engineering blamed finance. Nissan Europe accused Tokyo, and vice versa. The root of the problem was that the areas of executive responsibility were vague.[20]

The executive at Nissan explained that Ghosn's biggest gift to Nissan was replacing this "culture of blame" with a "commitment culture". Commitment means taking responsibility. It means dealing with problems, rather than putting them off. It means you have nowhere to hide and nobody else to blame when things go wrong… so you'd better make damn sure they go right. Without commitment, purpose, sacrifice and honesty, you can't create growth. Demonstrating an ability to make clear commitments and to follow through on these is fundamental to establishing credibility.

Commitment is an antidote to blame and "not invented here" syndrome. It prevents people merely talking about a business' purpose, and motivates them to actually act upon it. It confers a sense of moral obligation that financial incentivisation can't compete with. It's striking that Carlos Ghosn chose to make his own commitment so bold and public. In doing so, he deliberately created a point of no return: failure was no longer an option.

This is reminiscent of the ancient practice of armies burning bridges during military campaigns to render retreat impossible. Bridge burning also acted as a clear signal to opposing forces: if you want to beat us, you'll have to kill us first. The threat becomes more credible through an open demonstration of commitment. This is why open commitment is more powerful than commitments made in private. The ability to deliver on his rather outrageous profitability commitment sent a clear message to the rest of the business: if I can commit to turning around the entire company, you guys should be able to commit to doing your part to help me. Commitment becomes a two-way street. If the leader of a business makes a firm commitment to his employees, shareholders and customers, they are likely to reciprocate.

Demonstrating commitment in a different way, but using the proceeds of his company's success, Bill Gates goes a step further than the Microsoft organisation. The far-reaching Bill & Melinda Gates Foundation "works to help people lead healthy, productive lives. Focussing on the developing world on improving people's health, giving them the chance to lift themselves out of hunger and extreme poverty. In the US, it seeks to ensure that all people — especially those with the fewest resources — have access to the opportunities they need to succeed in school and life."[21] This activity and his approach demonstrate that commitment can reach outwards too.

In 2001, Robert Eisenberger and colleagues from the University of Delaware studied the roles of commitment and reciprocity in the context of an employer's relationship with his employees.[22] They administered a survey to 450 employees of a large mail processing facility in the Northeast United States and found that employee commitment, morale and performance were all positively affected by perceived organisational support – the employees' beliefs concerning how much the organisation values their contributions and cares about their wellbeing. In short: if an organisation openly demonstrates commitment to its employees, they will respond with higher levels of commitment and performance. And everyone will be happier as a result.

Narayana Hrudayalaya Hospitals
A pathway to affordable healthcare

When Mother Teresa suffered a heart attack in 1984, she received treatment at the BM Birla Hospital in Kolkata from Dr. Devi Shetty. It seems fair to say that Dr. Shetty is a doctor like no other.

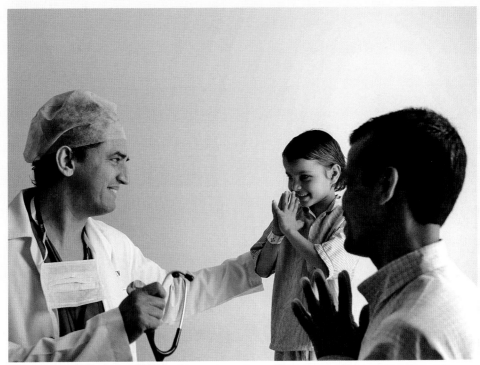

Courtesy of Narayana Hrudayalaya Hospitals

Part surgeon and part entrepreneur, he is the recipient of numerous awards for innovation from Ernst & Young, the Schwab Foundation and the Economist magazine. The Wall Street Journal has described Dr. Shetty as 'the Henry Ford of Heart Surgery'. In 2001 he built a massive cardiac centre outside Bangalore, aiming to bring down the cost of heart surgery to make it affordable to the poor as well as the rich. His mission is not simply to fix hearts but to fix the healthcare industry: *"There is something fundamentally wrong with the way healthcare is delivered. Less than 10% of the world's population can afford heart surgery. More than 90% of the world's population can't afford a heart operation, brain operation and other forms of essential, life-saving surgery. If the solution is not affordable, it is not a solution."*

In the space of little over a decade, Dr. Shetty's hospital has grown into a network of health centres called

Narayana Hrudayalaya. In the next seven years, the business expects to have 30,000 beds across India, Africa and Asia and aims to bring the cost of heart surgery down to a fraction of its current cost through greater economies of scale. There's something potentially alarming about this idea. Conventional wisdom suggests that a trade-off exists between quality and quantity. Higher prices and lower volumes signal better service. Lower prices and higher volumes imply that corners are being cut, which doesn't sound like a good idea when it comes to heart surgery. But Dr. Shetty doesn't believe in conventional wisdom. He knows better than that.

"The best way to reduce the cost of healthcare is by aiming for the highest quality. When you aim for quality, patients go home very fast, they are happy with the outcome and your cost goes down. Across the world the incidence of bedsores following heart operations is about 8%. For the last half-year we have been continuously having an occurrence of 0%. This is an example of how process change can impact the outcome. We have simple targets. Today we are able to do a major heart operation for $1,600 and break even. Our aim is to do the same operation for $800 and everyone is working towards that."

But Dr. Shetty's definition of quality isn't limited to hard measures of cost, bedsore incidence, mortality or morbidity. His definition of quality extends beyond successful operations. He prefers to think of his patients as customers and he is relentless in his pursuit of customer satisfaction. *"In this*

hospital we celebrate complaint. We encourage people to complain because when people complain, you know that something is not right and you can fix it. We have a system where everybody is encouraged to have a company-managed mobile phone on speed dial. So people can call that number and complain. And we used to get a few hundred complaints every day from various parts of the hospital. Now we have reduced it to about 100-150 complaints per day. And these complaints are registered and analysed and feedback is given. The intention is to constantly address the complaints. But we celebrate the complaints. We don't grumble about the complaints. You want to get better? Encourage people to complain."

Dr. Shetty is keen to point out that the feasibility of his business model relies upon a happy, motivated workforce. Happy employees matter as much as happy customers. At Narayana Hrudayalaya, motivation is about far more than money.

"The doctors are not scientists. They are artists. Outstanding doctors who have excelled in their area of interest tend to be very eccentric. We are able to understand them because we are one among them. So to that extent attracting and retaining talent is not that difficult. Nobody, unless they are eccentric, would be able to dedicate themselves to this profession, to be able to become an outstanding doctor. These kind of doctors, their wants and needs are totally different and to retain them, you have to give them something more. Money is not going to attract them. They are constantly looking for challenges, to do something different. So you have to create an environment where creative people can work and excel.

"But most of the people working in this hospital are not doctors, they are nurses, electricians and other employees. They

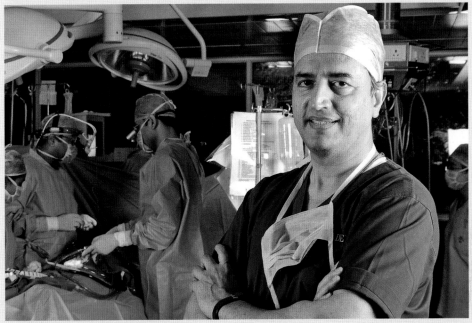

Courtesy of Narayana Hrudayalaya Hospitals

generally come from a lower economic background. They understand the value for low cost healthcare makes a difference. It is not difficult to motivate the people to work hard and excel in this industry because we are dealing with human life. We never refuse a patient. So they are very supportive because it is there to help their kind. Our employees know when their family members need any healthcare intervention; they can afford to come to our hospital. That is the difference. There is a sense of belonging. Once our employees have the feeling that this is their hospital, their entire attitude towards the customer changes. So it is very important that our employees are happy and that they believe in the mission for which the hospital was built."

Narayana Hrudayalaya's ability to continue to decrease the cost of healthcare depends on its ability to achieve scale, which in turn places heavy demands on finding and developing talent. Dr. Shetty is clear that he has an eye on the future as far as the next

generation of surgeons is concerned:
"We believe that all our hospitals have to be academic institutions wherein we take the future generation of surgeons, specialists and cardiologists. It's important because if you look across the world, institutions that are setting the standards for more than 20 years have invariably been academic institutions. We train young surgeons over a period of time. We not only train them by giving them the skills, we also develop their personalities. These surgeons are being trained by some of the best people in this business across the world. They are standing on the shoulders of giants. When these young people take over from us, we expect them to take the institution to a different level altogether because they are groomed by some of the best people in the business. So this is what we are looking at. And you can see the transformation happening."

"If you can reduce the cost of a heart operation, you can reduce the cost of anything."

Curiosity

Exercising imagination
Redefining convention
Encouraging challenge
Learning how to fail

Exercising imagination

Is knowledge really power? Around 3,000 years ago the Persian poet Ferdowsi expressed this sentiment in his literary epic, Shahnameh.[23] Ferdowsi was alive during the Bronze Age. Since then, the Iron Age, the Dark Ages, the Middle Ages and the Industrial Age have come and gone. Every age has its own version of imagination, but in each era, our imagination needs to be exercised. In the information age, the concept of knowledge as power has never seemed so pertinent, particularly in the world of business. According to a 2011 report by ESOMAR,[24] the global market research industry was worth US$31.2 billion in 2010, a growth of 2.8% in real terms. This means that our knowledge addiction is broadly the same size as General Motors (which at the time of writing has a market capitalisation of US$30.9 billion).

We've spent a lot of time working with market research and fully embrace the benefits it can deliver. Important decisions should be based on fact and not on pure sentiment. The market research industry has created some absolutely wonderful insight techniques, which can reveal deep truths about how we think, feel and behave towards businesses, their products, services and brands. But we've also seen enough to agree with the observation that many people in business use market research like a drunk uses a lamp post: for support rather than enlightenment. We've seen great market research go unnoticed, buried under a pile of absolutely useless claptrap. We've also seen millions of dollars squandered on information gathering where a combination of basic facts and common sense would have yielded a more reliable and sensible set of conclusions. It's a bad idea to make a decision with no information at all, but that doesn't mean that the best decisions are made with the most information.

Al Ries and Jack Trout wrote their marketing classic *Positioning: The battle for your mind* in 1976. The book was a result of the

authors' perception that society in the 1970s was overburdened with information (or "communication", in the authors' own words):

> Each year, some 30,000 books are published in America. Every year another 30,000. Which doesn't sound like a lot until you realize it would take 17 years of reading 24 hours a day just to finish reading one year's output... Take newspapers. Each year American newspapers use more than 10 million tons of newsprint. Which means that the average person consumes 94 pounds of newsprint a year... How much is getting through? ...Take television... The average American family is exposed to some 750,000 pictures a day. Not only are we being pictured to death, we are being papered to death... American business processes 1.4 trillion pieces of paper a year. That's 5.6 billion every working day.
>
> Who reads, sees, or listens to all this outpouring of communication?
>
> There's a traffic jam on the turnpikes of the mind. Engines are overheating. Tempers are rising.[25]

The problem with life in the information age is that there's so much information about. This predicament is even more acute nearly 40 years after Ries and Trout wrote their book. The internet has created an explosion in the amount of information available to us. According to an *Economist* article published in 2010, titled "Data, data everywhere",[26] our ability to generate information now exceeds the world's storage capacity.

It's easy to make sensible judgments with the benefit of hindsight, but success in business is a matter of foresight.

The article quotes a Cisco estimate that by 2013, the amount of traffic flowing over the internet annually will reach 667 Exabytes: a figure so enormous it's almost impossible to describe. Imagine each byte as a grain of sand. 667 Exabytes of sand could cover every beach on the planet nearly ninety times over.[27] Information overload is a far bigger issue for business than information scarcity. In the workplace, this has led to "analysis paralysis" – a diminished ability to make decisions, induced by an overload of emails, blogs, websites, mobile messaging, video conferencing, telephone conferencing and voicemail. Information doesn't feel like power any more. Its ubiquity has diminished its worth.

Overabundance isn't the only limit to information's power. Even with a complete and perfect understanding of the past and present, the future remains largely an unknown quantity. The key to tomorrow's growth is rarely found in yesterday's data. As Henry Ford (allegedly) said, "If I had asked people what they wanted, they would have said faster horses." The future is not a mere extrapolation of the past. It's easy to make sensible judgments with the benefit of hindsight, but success in business is a matter of foresight.

You can't create something unless you can first imagine it.

Business leaders make decisions about the future, not the past. Companies are valued based on the profits they are expected to deliver, not on the money already in the bank. As the cliché goes, "you can't drive a car by looking in the rear view mirror" (at least, not unless you're driving backwards). The ability to generate, store and manipulate information is only useful if it results in an educated guess about the future. In the words of Cecil Adams, "we know probability — certainty never".[28] When it comes to business, the ability to deal with uncertainty is a bigger challenge than how to deal with data. Power doesn't come from knowledge; it comes from making leaps of the mind into areas where knowledge cannot tread.

You can't create something unless you can first imagine it. This is one of the reasons some people compare entrepreneurs with artists: both need to establish a vision of something that does not yet exist. Imagination is the reason we aren't driving faster horses or using the sun to tell the time. Business can be sustained in the short-term through incremental improvements in the way we do things, based on knowledge of what works and doesn't work. But in the long-term, a greater level of invention is required. Innovation begins with an act of imagination: an ability to project ourselves beyond the world we know, to create hypotheses, to contemplate possibilities, to visualise opportunities, unencumbered by the limits of our knowledge.
This idea isn't as modern as it may seem. Albert Einstein is one of many prominent thinkers of the twentieth century to recognise the importance of imagination to problem-solving:

> Imagination is more important than knowledge. For knowledge is limited to all we now know and understand, while imagination embraces the entire world, and all there ever will be to know and understand.[29]

Napoleon Hill also believed in the power of imagination, but was more interested than Albert Einstein in its application to business and personal success, rather than solving the mysteries of the universe. Hill had been commissioned by industrialist Andrew Carnegie to interview over 500 millionaires, with the aim of developing (or, rather, confirming) a formula for success that

Carnegie had used to build his own fortune. Hill spent over twenty years on this mission and interviewed some of the twentieth century's most prominent Americans, including Henry Ford, William Wrigley Jr., George Eastman, Theodore Roosevelt, Charles Schwab, King Gillette, John D. Rockefeller, Thomas Edison, Woodrow Wilson and Dr. Alexander Graham Bell. Imagination was a central aspect of Hill's formula. Hill referred to imagination as "the workshop wherein are fashioned all plans created by man"[30] and distinguished between two types of imagination:

> *Synthetic imagination*: establishing novel connections between existing scraps of experience, education or observation, and
> *Creative imagination*: the hunches and moments of inspiration that result in completely new ideas.

As their names suggest, Hill championed creative imagination over synthetic imagination. We wouldn't necessarily go so far as this. James Dyson's invention of the world's first bagless vacuum cleaner was born from a frustration at loss of suction as traditional cleaner bags filled with dust and debris. While pondering this issue, Dyson noticed the cyclone in a nearby sawmill, which was used to spin sawdust out of the air, to be collected in a chamber. He applied the same principle to the problem of his vacuum cleaner, resulting in the launch of the DC01 – the first vacuum cleaner not to lose suction.

Necessity is the mother of invention and the godmother of imagination.

One of the most striking aspects of the DC01 was its clear bin: users would be able to see their vacuum cleaner filling up with dirt. Prior to launch in 1993, retailers and market research with potential users agreed that a clear bin would be a bad idea. At the time, this was an entirely novel concept and, so it seemed, entirely unnecessary and undesirable. James Dyson disagreed and history has proven him to be right: the DC01 was a runaway success and nearly every major vacuum cleaner company since has released a model featuring a clear bin.

The application of cyclone technology would have been dismissed as "synthetic" by Napoleon Hill, while he would have lauded the clear bin as a shining example of "creative" imagination. In retrospect, it seems fair to say that both aspects of the vacuum cleaner contributed to its success. The clear bin showcases the cyclone technology and provides visible evidence of the product's effectiveness. It demonstrates pride in the product and signals a radical departure from traditional vacuum cleaner design.

Unlike Napoleon Hill, we value both types of imagination, since synthesis and creativity are both helpful responses in situations of uncertainty. They enable us to break free of established modes of thought and patterns of behaviour, particularly when those modes and patterns are in danger of becoming tired and outdated. The Brazilians have a term for this capacity to circumvent convention with creativity: "jeito". The term roughly translates as "aptitude" or "knack" and is used to describe the ability to find ways around obstacles or problems. Just as Brazil's revered footballers demonstrate jeito as they dribble around opponents, the country's most admired businesses are applauded for finding creative and perhaps unconventional ways around challenges. Necessity is the mother of invention and the godmother of imagination.

Exercising imagination | Autolib'

Autolib'
Transforming mobility in Paris

Fifteen years ago, Paris City Council made a call for viable electric vehicle solutions that could be launched onto the streets of Paris. Industrialist Vincent Bolloré responded with a battery technology that no one had ever worked on before and won the bid to deliver Autolib', a fleet of zero-emission cars that had the potential to transform mobility in Paris.

Courtesy of Autolib'

Autolib' has been developed with a polymer metal lithium battery that stemmed from the workshops of Ergué-Gabéric in Bretagne. Before this, the majority of cars all over the world had been functioning with a thermal system.

Since its launch in December 2011, the project has delivered a clean, quiet and accessible transport alternative to millions of busy Parisians. It is admirable for its commitment to long-term

prosperity and investment in the future of the city. Autolib' may also be the birth of a model that can be replicated around the world in the future. We spoke to CEO of the electric car-sharing scheme, Morald Chibout, about the business and its growing success.

"You have to know that the first electric cars were launched only ten years ago. Bolloré is very bold as an entrepreneur, investing €1.5 billion from his own pocket and

progressively losing it until he succeeded in developing his project fifteen years later. Today, at Autolib' we have more than 71,000 subscribers and 28,000 of them are annual subscriptions, this is huge for such a project. We even reached 1,500,000 locations in the last few weeks. Since the launch in December 2011, it has been a real success, in a commercial but also mostly technological sense, since we managed to prove that the polymer metal lithium battery actually works – more than 1,500,000 people trusted us, rented the car and used it with its battery, onboard electronics and geolocalisation system."

"For the initial induction, users have direct contact with an advisor and five minutes later you have your subscription card in hand, and you can leave with a car. Our locations system allows you to book both your car and your place. This is really successful, especially on the new Internet version. You just need to book them at least 30 minutes before you need them. This system works 24/7, which is extraordinary and very convenient in a crowded city like Paris. The station 'recognises' each car, thanks to its embedded intelligence. No need to worry about finding a place to park anymore.

"Simplicity is both in your first steps with the brand and in the way you can use the location system and the car itself. I believe that a good product can be hard to build but easy to understand, the client should not feel any technical constraint."

Like with any project that is the first of its kind, there were a few initial teething problems while users became accustomed to the innovation. For example, Because 99% of existing cars are still six-speed cars, people sometimes feel a sense of apprehension when faced with an Autolib' vehicle.

Bolloré and his team pre-empted this and decided that with such a complex technological grounding, every other aspect of Autolib' must ooze simplicity. The reason why the exterior is simple is above all a design choice, and applying several layers of paint on it would have been in contradiction with their ecological vision. The car is a 'body-in-white' structure, without a single layer of paint. Simplicity, a sense of convenience and usability are also translated into the overall design of the vehicle.

"We had some troubles at first but these were mostly technical problems about how to use the car, because the electric car was still quite new last year. We saw some broken car bumpers, met people that couldn't open or close the car correctly; we even found a cat that was locked into a car. These are amusing anecdotes, but all in the past now. It wasn't the information system that caused problems – it was the car itself that was sometimes complicated for the clients. But today, they need less than thirty seconds to leave a parking station.

"What is captivating is the social and behavioural shift, going from a possession analysis to an analysis of use. French people are really close to their car, in the same way they are close to their house. They are a social representation and a means of expression for an individual. This concept of location is actually a true behavioural revolution. You do not own your car anymore, you rent it, you share it with other people but you can still have it anytime you need it.

"Clients like the way you can be part of the project, and the way you can easily move in Paris. What they love the most is the parking reservation system. You can easily go shopping at Faubourg Saint-Antoine by reserving your car 30 minutes in advance, and then coming back home and parking

Exercising imagination | Autolib'

Courtesy of Autolib'

your car in the closest station. There will always be a place for your car."

This technological revolution that started with a battery and ended with launching an eco-friendly car is radically transforming the way people consider mobility and move around in the city. The success of Autolib' is due to Bollore's ability to look forward and his approach to having a fully integrated project in order to keep control over it and avoid any dependence on other companies. Having an industrial background, Autolib' doesn't only develop the battery but also manufactures the other parts of the vehicles. This is undoubtedly a key part of the business' achievements so far and will contribute to its success in the future.

"We have received interest from the five continents, America, Asia, Africa etc. Everybody was thinking about this project,

but nobody had ever dared to launch it! In the future, we want to develop the model abroad. At the moment, our business model is based on Autolib' with the location and subscription system. It is fully viable: our president used to think it would break even in 2018 but now he claims that it will actually achieve it by the end of 2014 — three years ahead of time, due to its commercial success. Now that we've proved it is a viable model with its success in Paris, the idea is to launch it in other European and international capital cities. We are able to sell the car; the control system that is made by one of our subsidiaries, IER; and the information system is made by another of our subsidiaries, Polyconseil. We can also provide training for the call centres and management ambassadors.

"But at the same time we want to focus on developing our battery and keeping it at the core of our business. For us it's all about *energy storage, we are still working on the battery in order to improve the performance of our cars. Energy is a limited and vulnerable good; the proof is in the growing wind energy and alternative energy sector. The challenge is how to store energy. Once the storage problem is solved, the second challenge is to know how to re-inject it into the supply network. Some professions don't welcome a disruption in the energy market. For example, primary health insurance funds are thinking about hospital at home programmes, as it would be economic for them but such an idea cannot be created overnight. Yet our batteries are reactive to the nanosecond, and can easily connect EDF's grid power to your network, which would be relevant for this kind of application. Imagine, we could collect energy during the day with photovoltaics, store it in our batteries and then light up the streets at night."*

Exercising imagination is what triggered Autolib', 15 years ago, and is evidently what is leading it into the future.
The ambition and innovative thinking has created a business model that has the potential to transform city transport across the globe.

Redefining convention

Imagination can create significant value through disruptive products and service innovation, but it is also an enormous gamble. Dyson's DC01 wasn't created overnight. According to James Dyson, the cyclone technology for the DC01 took over 5,000 prototypes. It would require an enormous risk appetite for a business to focus solely on generating disruptive ideas that challenge and improve upon tried-and-tested ways of working. Innovation's hall of shame is bursting with examples of big gambles that didn't work out: Concorde, nuclear power, Betamax, laser discs, the DMC Delorean. This explains why there aren't many companies like Dyson in the world. The innovation process at many companies tends to focus on delivering a reliable stream of incremental improvements, rather than betting the farm on blockbuster ideas. This is why any supermarket aisle anywhere in the world is likely to carry at least one product that is new or improved.

Incremental, evolutionary, or "sustaining" innovation tends to be cheaper and is assumed to carry less risk of failure than more revolutionary ideas. Businesses can churn out "new and improved" products using the same factories, people and processes as before. But evidence demonstrates that incremental innovation fails just as much as disruptive innovation. It's difficult to find reliable data on the percentage of new products that fail, but figures quoted usually hover around the 75% to 80% mark. In a 2006 white paper on new product launches, Mark Sneider of AcuPOLL was even more pessimistic about this rate of failure: of 20,000 new products launched annually, Sneider found that "barely 10 percent" succeeded.[31] We all remember the big failures, but there are far, far more examples of failed evolutionary product ideas that probably made sense at the time: the Apple Lisa; Heinz purple and green EZ Squirt ketchup; Pepsi Blue; 3D Doritos; Supersize at McDonald's... The vast majority of these failures are incremental innovations, practical or easy – innovation with a small "i".

This is the "leaky bucket" approach to innovation. A pipeline of incremental innovation ideas is required because few – if any – of those innovations is realistically expected to survive beyond two years. This is why in innovation terms many businesses feel like they need to run in order to stand still. The 80-20 rule makes this approach possible: 80% of sales are likely to come from a core set of established products and services, which means that the failure of a couple of recently introduced marginal products and services won't critically damage sales. The failure rate may be high but the stakes are low... at least in the short-term. In the longer-term, the leaky bucket innovation approach doesn't seem quite so harmless. Companies' finite resources are invested in innovation that won't exist after three years, at the expense of more fundamental, revolutionary ideas that have greater potential to sustain business in the long run. Of the original 1955 Fortune 500 companies, only sixty-six remain on the list today — a drop-off rate of over seven companies each year. This rate is increasing: only 283 of the current list were Fortune 500 companies ten years ago — a drop-off rate of over twenty-one companies a year over the past decade. Cursory analysis of the companies that have disappeared reveals some common themes. Some companies — Dynegy, Enron, MCI WorldCom, Lehman Brothers — represent a rogue's gallery of businesses that have failed to act with integrity.

A second group includes companies such as Motorola, Northwest Airlines, Gateway and Levi Strauss, which have failed to anticipate smartphones, low-cost airlines, build-to-order direct computer manufacture and the rise of fast fashion, respectively. These are paradigm shifts in how categories work, how companies sell and how customers buy. The problem is not that these companies failed to invest in innovation: Motorola had developed the world's first GPRS network and phone; Northwest was the first US passenger airline to offer internet check-in; Levi's have pioneered commuter clothing. The problem was that they neglected to innovate their own business models, as well as innovating their products and services.

A lack of sufficient curiosity about the future limits our ability to identify opportunity and to avoid obsolescence.

This isn't an argument against incremental innovation: it is absolutely essential to the lifecycle of a product or service line that it should evolve over time to deliver additional benefits and to reflect changing needs. But incremental innovation should be balanced with the more fundamental re-imagination of a company's business model, driven by a combination of insight and foresight into customer needs and underlying political, economic, environmental, social and technological trends. A lack of sufficient curiosity about the future limits our ability to identify opportunity and to avoid obsolescence. We can't predict the future, but this doesn't mean we can't anticipate it. Nike understands the importance of "big" innovation. Hoovers, the company information service, describes Nike as a "maker of athletic footwear and apparel". But Nike doesn't limit itself to such a narrow definition of its business. While the company invests heavily in innovative technology to create better-performing sportswear (Nike has over 6,000 patents), its bigger commitment is to deliver "inspiration and innovation for every athlete in the world". In 1987, Nike launched the "Nike Monitor": a brown plastic box about the size of a paperback book, which used sonar detectors to help a runner track his speed and distance travelled. The product was dropped from Nike's range less than two years later, but the same idea has resurfaced more recently as Nike+. Launched in collaboration with Apple in 2006, the basic premise was the same: instead of a cumbersome box, runners could use their iPod to track the distance and speed of their runs. In its first incarnation, Nike+ required the user to purchase a sensor with an in-built accelerometer that could be inserted in a specially made range of Nike running shoes. This sensor would transmit data to the runner's iPod, which could then be synced through iTunes to create a history, set challenges and share with friends through social networking platforms.

At some point, it becomes necessary for a business to contemplate seriously what "different" might look like.

This first incarnation of Nike+ was only a tentative step away from Nike's core business. The sensor required a dedicated running shoe, so Nike+ could be described as an evolution of Nike's "running hardware". But the advent of the GPS-enabled iPhone eliminated the need for a sensor altogether, which meant that a dedicated shoe was no longer necessary. If Nike had thought of itself solely as a sports equipment manufacturer, then Nike+ would no longer have been an interesting proposition. But the people at Nike realized that Nike+ had fundamentally changed their relationship with runners: rather than being peripheral to the running experience, Nike+ had placed their business at its heart.

Since launch, Nike+ has established a virtual community of around 5 million runners, where people can share their runs and challenge themselves and each other to run faster, longer and harder. According to the Nike+ website, the system has resulted in the running of 621 million miles, as well as contributing to an incremental US$608 million in non-equipment and apparel sales last year. This is still small change for a company with revenues of US$24 billion, but the recent addition of the Nike+ FuelBand demonstrates that this could evolve into a multi-billion dollar opportunity, twenty-five years after the launch of the Nike Monitor.

Making "better" products will only take a business so far. Over time, tried-and-tested business models become easier to repli-cate and more difficult to improve upon through incremental innovation. At some point, it becomes necessary for a business to contemplate seriously what "different" might look like. In the long-term, growth depends on a business' ability to re-imagine itself for the future. The surviving members of the original 1955 Fortune 500 have demonstrated a wonderful knack for re-imagination. In 1955, Thomas J. Watson Jr. was three years into his presidency and only just beginning to refocus IBM from a manufacturer of measurement and tabulation machines toward the development and commercialisation of electronic computer technology. GE had only just invented the world's first truly automatic portable dishwasher. Over the intervening years, these businesses have re-imagined their business models, without losing sight of their purpose. In doing so, they have introduced new ways of doing things and challenged the rest of the business community to keep up.

Redefining convention | Icebreaker

Icebreaker
A new relationship with nature

When Jeremy Moon founded Icebreaker, he was twenty-four, broke and had absolutely no idea what he was doing. He was driven by a passion for what he saw was possible, and a belief that he could make it happen. That ambition was ignited in a meeting with a merino sheep farmer.

Courtesy of Icebreaker

"Across the dining table, he threw me a t-shirt made from merino wool fabric he'd designed himself. It felt soft and sensuous and nothing like regular wool. The shirt could be washed in the washing machine rather than by hand; it was silky and soft rather than itchy, and it felt light instead of heavy. I thought, 'Wow! This is an amazingly beautiful, practical, natural material. This is a product I could sell around the world.'

With a mantra at the time of "this will work if I don't screw it up", Moon used a paper he had written for his master's degree at the University of Otago titled "Why Businesses Fail", to work out how "not to screw it up".

"I remember three things: one they ran out of capital; two — they didn't have sufficient management experience; and three — they had an undifferentiated product and ended up having to compete just on price.

"I raised $200,000 from eight investors to ensure we had the initial capital that we needed — enough to get us going but not too much to make me lazy or feel like the business was a success before the right was earned.

"Secondly, I set up a board of directors as I had no management experience, limited life experience and needed some grey hair around me to balance my passion and testosterone. They taught me how to think long-term, how to plan, how to build teams, and helped me sharpen my decision-making.

"The third area was the choice of how we invested the capital. I invested over half into the design of the brand and the rest into the design of the product."

Moon's investments paid off: customers returned for more of the long-lasting, comfortable, durable and distinctive products that could justify the premium price tags as "merino isn't cheap".

"For me, I'm not interested in just making and selling clothes. I want to create meaning that is based on truth and is executed to a high standard. My training originally was in cultural anthropology and my obsession is around the meaning that we as humans give to objects. As humans we are meaning machines, we attach meaning to everything, and the objects that

we bring into our lives are congruent with our sense of self and reflect either who we are or who we want to be.

"When I launched Icebreaker in the mid-90s we targeted the snow sports, outdoor and adventure clothing market. The brands that were dominant then were all telling variations of the same story — 'sweaty men climbing mountains as quickly as possible'. We did the opposite. We made it about men and women, and we made it about kinship with nature, rather than conquering it. And then we offered the choice — wearing nature in nature instead of synthetics made from petrochemicals, which defined the outdoor clothing industry. We zigged when they were zagging. That instantly made us different and intriguing, we had a product that could back it up and a true story of a fibre born in the mountains.

"It seemed counterintuitive at the time, but I was using the same superfine merino wool that was in a $3000 Italian suit to make thermal underwear for people to sweat in. The price of Icebreaker was twice the price of competitor products made from cheap synthetics. Therefore a premium brand and a differentiated story was critical, not only to differentiate us but also to earn the price point we required. The brand had to be seductive and engage on an emotional level, and my bet was that the 'born in nature worn in nature' meaning would connect with people at an intrinsic level; because as we all huddle in cities and get progressively disconnected from nature, the metaphor of wearing nature everyday helps to close that gap."

The commitment at Icebreaker to make things of quality and something to be proud of has resulted in the details of every aspect of their products being laboured over.

Courtesy of Icebreaker

"An example is when we were creating our packaging system for our base layer product. The packaging has gone on to win major design awards and looks elegant, beautiful and simple, but it took fourteen iterations before I gave it my final approval. Sometimes my perfectionism around these little issues can drive our design team a little crazy, but my stand is to create fully resolved products for our customers. Quest for perfectionism is what defines a design-led company and a leader of a market segment."

The respect and love of the outdoors is inherent in the Icebreaker products to the staff that work there. Icebreaker's enthusiasm in bridging the gap between nature and people is contagious when customers buy the products.

"The original meaning of Icebreaker is about ice breaking between people and between people and nature — it's about new relationships. This is unlimited territory and relates to the whole meaning of life so we're not going to run out of inspiring

stories to tell. It's really about how we tell them and how our clothing reflects these true stories.

"We receive endless comments through our social media channels on how our merino clothing has changed their lives. People want to share their experiences with us. We received a hilarious email from a guy in Scotland who wore one of our t-shirts in Egypt for seven days, after losing his luggage. On his return, his top blew off the washing line at home and he was devastated but his conclusion was: 'What have I learnt? Advertising hype isn't always hype. Icebreaker merino is weird sh!t. I need to start a fund for a new top as unfortunately weird sh!t does not come cheap."

Working hard to ensure that Icebreaker products justify the use of such an expensive material has allowed the company to steadily grow and sell the brand in more than 3,000 outdoor and sport stores across forty-four countries; however, this level of success comes with a new set of challenges.

"I am sometimes frustrated with how our brand is presented in these stores, compared with the vision that we have and the story that we know is there. That's why, over the last three years, we have made a deep commitment to grow our own retail and online business in addition to our wholesale business. We also now have a thriving online business globally. This is very exciting for us, as we now have a direct conversation path to our customers."

While many companies are beginning to replicate the Icebreaker business model, a direct relationship with customers seems vital for the company to successfully communicate its purpose with clarity.

"We are working together collaboratively to chisel back what has made Icebreaker great in the past and take that into the future with our online, retail and wholesale businesses. I feel the next wave of Icebreaker is being born right now. We have a transparent supply chain and the highest environmental, ethical and social standards. Our objective is profitable sustainability."

The impact that Icebreaker has on people when they encounter their products or stories is what will continue the appeal of a natural choice in an age of synthetics. This is where the passion began and what will continue to motivate Moon in the future.

"Early on someone said to me that when you're setting up a small business you have more highs and lows in one month than most people have in a year, and that was certainly true. It made me feel hugely alive being challenged on every level — a start-up demands 100% from every cell in your body. It's relentless and exhausting but worth it, and only the strongest survive. I admire all entrepreneurs who have won or who have failed."

Photograph by Ty Cole, courtesy of Icebreaker

Encouraging challenge

There's a danger in integrity; it all too easily slips into languor. A fine line exists between unwavering commitment to principle and inflexibility. History is littered with businesses that have failed to respond to a changing world: Kodak, Polaroid, Blockbuster... Air Wales (which proves no business is too big to fail). Success in business is largely about being able to deal with change, to see opportunity where others see only challenge.

The business world likes to worship its heroes. Titans of business, like Steve Jobs, Richard Branson and Bill Gates are admired as visionaries. But it isn't healthy or sustainable for businesses to rely on the talents of a few great minds to drive innovation and change. Inflexibility, close-mindedness and inertia are cultural issues. The ability of a business to adapt and thrive in the face of change relies on the extent to which it can foster a culture of restlessness, challenge and openness to opportunity.

Brand consultants are fond of talking about the importance of cultural alignment. Their vision of the perfect business is one in which employees behave in accordance with a prescribed set of values, which projects a clear and consistent image to the outside world. This is the notion of brand as a "central organizing principle" and explains why reception areas around the world are plagued with framed posters that contain an identikit set of codes and behaviour, such as "accountability" and "transparency" and "excellence". We have yet to see a business that genuinely lives up to this ideal, which is almost certainly a good thing. Innovative businesses don't prioritise control and order at the expense of entrepreneurialism and agility. Change requires challenge.

How can a business organise itself to be more imaginative? Creativity, imagination and innovation are impossible to enforce through a system of processes or rules. In a 2007 paper titled "Creating and Sustaining a Winning Culture" three Bain & Company partners shared the results of a worldwide survey of 1,200 senior executives, 91% of whom agreed that "culture is as important as strategy for business success". The article places a significant emphasis on achieving cultural alignment. In the first place, this means working with senior management to create a "single voice" for the entire organisation. In the second place, this involves aligning "hard drivers" such as organisational structure, talent management systems and incentives to make sure the culture is embedded for the long-term.

None of this seems controversial. Strong cultural alignment results in a more harmonious working environment and helps to coordinate employee behaviour and decision-making. Management theorists prefer the tool of culture to a formal system of rules because it is a more positive way to inspire behaviour, rather than overtly seeking to control it. Rules also rob employees of their ability to take responsibility for their actions, whereas culture places the onus on individuals to be accountable and responsible for their own decisions and actions. Harmony, it seems, is best achieved through the exercise of "soft power".

But is harmony really such a good thing? Is agreement more valuable to a business than disagreement? And does a productive culture really require such a high level of consensus? The Bain report also quotes an interesting statistic from another of its studies: 81% of executives agree that a company without a winning culture is "doomed to mediocrity". Mediocrity isn't something any business aspires to. It's something that businesses allow to happen. And it is frequently the result of an over-emphasis on harmony and consensus in decision-making. Part of the reason is that people often only pretend to agree with one another. Harmony is a seductive idea in theory, but in practice it relies on a combination of indifference, surrender, submission to authority and compromise. None of these is an attribute of effective or brave decision-making. Compromise in particular is a sure-fire route to mediocrity. Intelligent people are more likely than not to disagree on important issues. It is far

Mediocrity isn't something any business aspires to. It's something that businesses allow to happen.

better to encourage open discussion of their different views than to compel consensus through culture. The Bain partners' conclusions are particularly striking given the culture of Bain & Co itself. According to the company's own website, "we seek multiple points of view to ensure that we have the best answers for our clients. An open mind to new information helps us improve our ideas."

Bain isn't alone in championing debate over consensus. Some of the world's most innovative organisations are even more bullish about the value of dissent and diversity of opinion. PayPal is one such company. Set up after a chance meeting at Stanford University, Peter Thiel and Max Levchin created their first electronic wallet proposition in 1998, which evolved into PayPal in 1999. From the beginning, PayPal's founders were preoccupied with fostering a culture that was strong but by no means orthodox or harmonious. Their belief was that the talent of individuals should not be held back by consensus or alignment. The organisation was antipathetic to meetings — gatherings of more than four people were viewed with caution and subject to immediate adjournment if they weren't deemed to be productive. Disruptive behaviour was required, not discouraged. Jeremy Stoppelman, now CEO of Yelp, tells the following story[32] from his time at PayPal:

I was a 22-year-old whippersnapper, and I remember firing off this email that disagreed with the entire executive staff. I didn't get fired – I got a pat on the back.

Crucially, there was an expectation within the company that important issues would attract intense debate. The ability to defend a clear point of view – backed by evidence – was expected of anybody with a contribution to make. Dissent is easy to dismiss as dangerous and destructive if we assume that people within businesses are driven by prejudice and that opposing points of view can be resolved only through compromise. But if differences of opinion are encouraged – as long as they are backed by reason and openly discussed – then this encourages people in a business to make a clear and compelling argument for change. Even low-level employees were encouraged to question decisions and to come up with their own suggestions for improvement. And if the data didn't exist to justify a hunch, then people were encouraged to test their hunch – on the understanding that they would be responsible for the outcome and may have to retreat from their position if success failed to materialise.

Harmony is a seductive idea in theory, but in practice it relies on a combination of indifference, surrender, submission to authority and compromise.

Jeremy Stoppelman isn't the only ex-PayPal employee to advocate the importance of dissonance in driving innovation. David Sacks was employed as PayPal's Chief Operating Officer and subsequently founded Yammer in 2008. In a 2011 interview with the New York Times,[33] Sacks reiterated the importance of a democratic culture, where dissent is valued:

I think you've got to create a culture in which dissent is valued. And there's probably a lot of ways to set that tone. Certainly you can tell if you've got a culture of dissent when you walk into a company. People can figure out very quickly whether dissent is encouraged or whether it's actually something that's not welcome.

It's a red flag to me if there's just too much consensus and not enough dissent. I feel like in any human community there's always dissent because people just disagree. Anytime there doesn't appear to be dissent, it means that the corporate culture has just shifted way too much toward consensus. That means the leadership just doesn't welcome dissent enough.

Encouraging dissent is a way of letting employees know that management is curious about and willing to act upon their opinion. The people who work for you are as well placed as anybody to identify when your strategy isn't up to scratch. The corollary of demonstrating this curiosity is that employees are in turn encouraged to be curious about the business and what it can achieve. If your voice can't be heard in a business then there's little incentive to take an interest in its future. If you have the ability to air your views, this creates a very strong reason to make sure that your point is well informed, well articulated and well intentioned, because the CEO is likely to find out about it. Cultural strength isn't measured by the level of agreement achieved within a company; it is measured by a business' ability to accommodate a diversity of people and opinions without falling over.

Former IBM chairman Thomas Watson, Jr. understood how important it was to encourage people to challenge the status quo within a business. He coined the term "wild ducks" to describe employees who don't fit in with the prevailing culture of the company. He saw these employees as a "priceless ingredient" for IBM. The term "wild duck" is borrowed from a parable by Danish philosopher Soren Kierkegaard:

> With his mates, a wild duck was flying in the Springtime northward across Europe. During the flight he came down in a Danish barnyard where there were tame ducks. He ate of their corn and liked it. He stayed for an hour – then for a day – then a week – then a month – and finally, because he relished the good fare and the safety of a barnyard, he stayed all summer. Then one Autumn day when the flock of wild ducks was winging its way southward again, it passed over the barnyard and their mate heard their cries. His breast stirred with a great thrill of joy and delight, and with a great flapping of wings, he rose in the air to join his old comrades in their flight but he found that his good fare had made him fat and his muscles so soft and flabby that he could no longer rise higher than the eaves of the barn. So he dropped back into the barnyard and said to himself, "Oh, well, my life is safe here and the food is good." But, alas, he was not safe from the man who fed him, for he later discovered that he was being fattened for the kill.[34]

The moral of the story for Watson was that you can make a wild duck tame, but once tamed, the duck can never become wild again. He also took to heart the point that a tame duck will never go anywhere. A retired IBM employee described Watson's emphasis on "wild ducks" in a letter to the New York Times in 1989:

> I first heard it in the mid-1960s when I was a young IBM-er in NY. Thomas J. Watson Jr., then chairman, was speaking to employees in a telephone broadcast. Here is the part about wildfowl: "I talk a lot around here about wild ducks, and people

Encouraging dissent is a way of letting employees know that management is curious about and willing to act upon their opinion.

kid me a good deal about my wild ducks. But it takes a few wild ducks to make any business go, because if you don't have the fellows with the new ideas willing to buck the managerial trends and shock them into doing something new and better, if you don't have those kind of people, the business pretty well slows down. So I would tell a 21-year-old IBM-er what I've told a lot of 21-year-old college people... that is, that the priceless ingredient that a youngster has when he starts in business is that sense of not compromising beyond a certain point.[35]

3M
A culture of invention

3M is a global innovation company
that never stops inventing. Founded in 1902 at the
Lake Superior town of Two Harbors, Minnesota, five
businessmen set out to mine a mineral deposit for
grinding-wheel abrasives.

Courtesy of 3M

The deposits proved to be of little value, and the new Minnesota Mining and Manufacturing Company moved to nearby Duluth to focus on sandpaper products.

Like many others in the early 1900s, 3M's founders incorporated first and investigated later. In the face of failure, they persevered and turned their investment into a lucrative venture. New investors were attracted to 3M, such as Lucius Ordway, who moved the company to St. Paul in 1910. Early technical and marketing innovations began to produce successes.

3M's Corporate Research Laboratory was founded in 1937, recently celebrating its 75th anniversary in St Paul. We spoke to Dr Larry Wendling the global Research Laboratory's Vice President, who joined 3M because of its reputation in science and technology. He pointed out: "The principles of 3M are the same today as they were from the beginning – it's a business, not a university. Our solutions are not ivory tower solutions." And he refers to the researchers as 'blue-collar scientists'.

"3M is fundamentally a science-based company. We produce thousands of imaginative products, and we're a leader

in scores of markets — from healthcare and highway safety to office products and abrasives and adhesives. Our success begins with our ability to apply our technologies — often in combination — to an endless array of real-world customer needs. Of course, all of this is made possible by the people of 3M and their singular commitment to make life easier and better for people around the world.

"Over the years, our innovations have improved daily life for hundreds of millions of people all over the world. We have made driving at night easier, made buildings safer, and made consumer electronics lighter, less energy intensive and less harmful to the environment. We even helped put a man on the moon. Every day at 3M, one idea always leads to the next, igniting momentum to make progress possible around the world. Technology and R&D are right in the middle of the business, and the 3M business model is innovation, that's what creates value in the company.

As Dr Wendling says "Our culture helps us to stand apart, especially the mutual respect between our scientists and laboratories and the rest of the business. Networking is a huge factor. We set up a professional society in 1951 to connect all the labs, and there are over 800 events a year to link the groups together. We cover all areas of science including nanotechnology and biotechnology. Our senior researchers hand down expertise to newer staff, who add their own individual contributions to their technology platform, advance the technology and then pass it on to the next generation. It's all about balance, an ecosystem of scientists connected by innovation to manufacturing, customer service, supply chain and other parts of the business. We work years ahead in development, and we thrive on the diversity of the product range. We're always looking for breakthroughs in new ideas and the reinforcement of existing ideas and products — making them stronger, longer lasting."

A key part of the culture at 3M is their Bootlegging Policy, which allows their technical employees to spend up to 15% of their time developing their own creative ideas for the company — where they can explore ideas for innovative products or services that might benefit the company. This is central to 3M's global innovation, and is supported by their Genesis Grant programme, to take ideas forward — if any ideas generated in Bootlegging time look viable, the next step is to assess if for funding through the Genesis Grant programme. There are many successes from the Bootlegging Policy, the most famous is the Post-it note, but they include clear bandages, optical films that reflect light, designing a way to make painter's tape stick to wall edges, all of which are on the market now. And Dr Wendling himself still uses his 15% time.

The investment in R&D at 3M is mighty. *"We have a metric on new product development."* Dr Wendling told us *"initiated in 1988, this measures new product revenues as a percentage of total revenues, we call it the new product vitality index. Our target is 35 to 40% of revenues, short cycle (eg electronics) is higher, long cycle (eg healthcare) is lower, but averages are spot on."*

Dr Wendling also told us a couple of stories that demonstrate development opportunity in action. 3M tackled the challenge of transmitting more electrical power over existing high voltage towers by developing new high voltage power cables based on ceramic fibers versus conventional steel cables. The standard cables sag more from heating than the ceramic as more power is transmitted through the cable. The new ceramic cable can transmit two to three times the electrical power of conventional cables. The core is stranded from wires of high purity aluminum reinforced with alumina fibers.

The outer, current carrying wires are a hardened aluminum zirconium alloy. The resulting conductor has the same strength as similar size steel core conductors, but is much lighter and sags less. It also retains its performance over decades of high temperature use, and is stable in a wide range of environmental conditions.[36] The ACCR cable has been installed to solve challenging issues around the world, including long-span river crossings and extra high voltage and renewable energy installations.

"We also make glass spheres, used in things like reflective coatings, the paint in road markings etc. Every so often we would accidently produce a hollow ball. We tried to think of ways in which these little balls might be made useful. It turns out they are really useful for insulation, used to insulate deep sea oil pipes Another example is the use of microrepliction technology to develop brightness enhancement films used in LCD displays. When microreplication technology was first developed in the 1960's, we had no idea that it would be put to such a use. It is deeply gratifying to see research and technology applied to real world problems. Scientists and engineers are motivated by applying their technological achievements to problems. In order for that to happen, you need to know the problems you are solving - I think that is where the curiosity comes in."

Dr Wendling sees the biggest challenge and opportunity for 3M is retaining the balance of leading-edge innovation and sustainable business for the future, and maintaining this through an extensive corporate memory attitude where values are handed down, added to and built on. From what we know about 3M, they can do this through their thirst for solutions and the culture of encouraging challenge that their employees seem to thrive on.

Learning how to fail

There's a rousing scene in Ron Howard's 1995 movie "Apollo 13" in which Ed Harris plays the role of Gene Kranz, NASA's Flight Director, working desperately with his team to figure out how to bring the flight crew home safely following the explosion of a service module. Emotions are running high. American lives are at risk. The team are discussing never-before-attempted scenarios to get their boys home, against all the odds. At the conclusion of the conversation, Gene Kranz galvanises his team with the concluding statement, "failure is not an option". These are bold words. We frequently hear them repeated in the world of business — sometimes in an abbreviated form as "FNAO". Failure is to be avoided at all cost. Processes must be robust. Methodologies must be tried and tested. Certainty must be delivered.

The problem is that none of this is actually true. Gene Kranz never uttered those words. They were dreamed up by the movie's scriptwriters, following a conversation with Flight Controller Jerry Bostick in which he explained:

> When bad things happened, we just calmly laid out all the options, and failure was not one of them. We never panicked, and we never gave up on finding a solution.[37]

There's a big difference between stating that "failure is not an option" and the more reasonable approach to problem-solving described above. FNAO is used by businesses to communicate a zero-tolerance approach to failure. This suggests that sources of failure should be eradicated and that any instances of failure should be seen as a source of shame for the business, potentially prompting an inquiry into who is to blame and signalling subsequent unemployment for the poor soul who didn't get the FNAO memo. But sound-bites that sound great in Tom Hanks movies rarely translate into sensible management principles (life is like a box of chocolates?). Jerry Bostick's summary of NASA's approach to making decisions in a crisis seems altogether more positive than FNAO: when bad things happen, don't let failure distract you from identifying positive strategies for success. Failure is inevitable. Promoting a fear of making mistakes won't stop them from happening. At best, it makes people risk-averse. At worst, it stifles creativity and encourages people to cover up mistakes until cracks become too large to paper over.

Lack of failure comes at a significant cost: lack of innovation. It's extremely difficult to launch new propositions or to intro-duce new ways of working without taking a leap into the unknown. The bolder the initiative, the braver the initiator. Com-panies like PayPal, Nike and Dyson have all experienced failure, but failure at these companies is regarded as an opportunity to learn. Failing itself is not a crime, but failing to learn certainly is. People in these companies aren't punished for pushing boundaries to unlock new opportunities for growth. Failure is an investment in future success. As Edward Albee said, "If you're willing to fail interestingly, you tend to succeed interestingly."[38]

Google champions failure to the extent that it is willing to flaunt its flops in public. At a conference in 2010, Google's CEO Eric Schmidt proudly announced, "We celebrate our failures". A review of the company's history of product launches shows that Google must celebrate with Bacchanalian frequency. Schmidt's announcement followed the failure of Google Wave, a next-generation messaging system designed to make email redundant. In the same year, Google also saw the failure of SearchWiki, which allowed people to shape their Google search results manually. Both projects seem to have disappointed because of the perception that they added complexity to an experience people valued for its simplicity. In 2009, Google celebrated at least seven prominent failures, including Google Catalogs, Google Notebook and Google Video. In 2011, Google Health and Google TV failed to perform as expected and attracted significant media attention. As Marissa Mayer explained at The Fortune Most Powerful Women Summit in 2011, "It's totally fine to fail, you just have to fail fast."[39]

Failing itself is not a crime, but failing to learn certainly is.

But this attitude doesn't seem to take failure at all seriously. Failure is allowed to happen because none of these projects individually matters. The 80-20 rule re-enters the stage. Google engineers spend 80% of their time working on the core business and are encouraged to spend 20% of their time on something company-related that interests them personally. The stability of Google's core business – married with the sheer number of ideas its 30,000 engineers must be spending 20% of their time working on – means that nobody needs to worry if individual ideas fail. Schmidt himself explained in an interview with Forbes in 2011 that, "At the launch, the trick is not to get expectations too high." Low expectations at launch mean that Google doesn't need to engage in too much soul-searching when things go wrong. "Fast failure" means that they can quickly move on to the next idea. Failure becomes tolerated as a form of innovation waste.

Every innovation project should matter and failure should always hurt. Google's "fast" innovation process seems to favour quickly moving on from failure, instead of taking the time to learn from it. There's little outward evidence of introspection. And Google seems to abandon the "fast fail" model when it really matters. Despite claims it has made to the contrary, Google+ is widely viewed as Google's response to Facebook (and is described in these terms by ex-Google employees). This is a challenge that the "fast failure" model had failed at... fast. But the threat from Facebook to Google's core business — advertising revenue — isn't going away. So as far as Google+ is concerned, failure is no longer an option.

Every innovation project should matter and failure should always hurt.

A recent blog titled "Why I left Google", posted by James Whittaker, a former Googler, offers an insider's view of the recent change in emphasis of their innovation model:

> Ideas that failed to put Google+ at the center of the universe were a distraction. Suddenly, 20% meant half-assed... As the trappings of entrepreneurship were dismantled, derisive talk of the "old Google" and its feeble attempts at competing with Facebook surfaced to justify a "new Google" that promised "more wood behind fewer arrows."

> The days of old Google hiring smart people and empowering them to invent the future was gone. The new Google knew beyond doubt what the future should look like. Employees had gotten it wrong and corporate intervention would set it right again.

> Officially, Google declared that "sharing is broken on the web" and nothing but the full force of our collective minds around Google+ could fix it. You have to admire a company willing to sacrifice sacred cows and rally its talent behind a threat to its business. Had Google been right, the effort would have been heroic and clearly many of us wanted to be part of that outcome. I bought into it. I worked on Google+ as a development director and shipped a bunch of code. But the world never changed; sharing never changed. It's arguable that we made Facebook better, but all I had to show for it was higher review scores.

> As it turned out, sharing was not broken. Sharing was working fine and dandy, Google just wasn't part of it. People were sharing all around us and seemed quite happy. A user exodus from Facebook never materialized. I couldn't even get my own teenage daughter to look at Google+ twice, "social isn't a product," she told me after I gave her a demo, "social is people and the people are on Facebook." Google was the rich kid who, after having discovered he wasn't invited to the party, built his own party in retaliation. The fact that no one came to Google's party became the elephant in the room.[40]

Being too tolerant of failure can be just as damaging as being too intolerant. "Fast failing" works fine when the stakes are low and your customers are willing to be treated like guinea pigs. Most businesses aren't in this situation. Failure hurts. But innovative companies understand that while failure can be managed, it can't be eliminated altogether. Celebrating failure encourages an "anything goes" attitude to innovation. On the other hand, stigmatising failure results in the kind of cover-ups that over time turn small problems into colossal crises. Failure is most healthily regarded as a harsh but valuable lesson in business. In the process of developing a commercially viable lightbulb, Thomas Edison is reputed to have created 10,000 unsuccessful prototypes. I'm willing to bet he didn't celebrate each time. But he did learn from each disappointment:

> I have not failed 10,000 times. I have not failed once. I have succeeded in proving that those 10,000 ways will not work. When I have eliminated the ways that will not work, I will find the way that will work.[41]

These words echo the pragmatic approach to failure described by Jerry Bostick. Failure shouldn't be feared any more than it should be fetishized. Setbacks and disappointments are both painful and inevitable in the course of trying out new ways of doing business. We can admire people like Thomas Edison because he failed systematically: failing, learning and then trying something different; never repeating the same mistake twice; continuing to learn until he had achieved his goal.

Learning how to fail | Interface

Interface
Achieving mission zero

In 1994, Ray Anderson, owner and founder of carpet manufacturing company Interface, pledged to eliminate any negative impact it had on the environment by 2020.

Courtesy of Interface

We spoke to Sustainability Director, Ramon Arratia about how Ray's charm, charisma and skills of persuasion led the company through a redesign of processes and products; the use of new technologies; and the elimination of waste and harmful emissions, all while increasing the use of renewable materials and energy sources. This revolution was titled 'Mission Zero'.

Anderson was determined to work with sustainability experts such as Janine Benyus, Paul Hawkens, Amory Lovins and Jonathon Porritt to generate ideas in how to change the business. One of the most successful outcomes was the, 'idea of bio mimicry, arranging the carpet tiles so that they resembled the ideals of nature. That was a hugely successful commercial product.'

Whilst working towards total sustainability, it became evident that very few companies could show that a business could be sustainable and profitable at the same time. Interface intended to remain a business and had no intention of becoming a charity.

"We are a very aggressive company — we want to make a very strong profit but also achieve our pledge to eliminate our environmental impact by 2020. So it is a combination of traditional aggressive corporate behaviour for profit, coupled with a clear goal."

With a mission to change how the business worked, Interface also decided to be 'the example for other companies', they intended 'to show other companies that having zero environmental impact was possible.'

"We work with consultants, giving our knowledge for free so that they can use that to help their clients. Every year we take some consultants to Holland for two days, they can bring their clients if they want. We call it the 'Cultural Immersion Programme'. Basically, we are trying to give everything we have learned about sustainability so that others can profit from it."

Interface focuses on differentiating itself from competitors with clarity and openness. They do this by helping customers make informed decisions by stating facts and not making claims.

"We won't go out and call a product eco-lease and our competitors will. We don't go out and say that our products are sustainable by so much. We just give the facts — for example 'this product has 5 kilos of CO2'. That candidness, customers really appreciate. We are just giving facts. My department spends half its time

developing sustainable products and then the other half thinking of how we can best communicate and bring it to the market, either through marketing materials, the sales force or opinion leaders."

Following the success of the bio-mimicry carpet, Interface invented a new 100% recycled nylon carpet that came with its own story to tell.

"This is made from some of our old carpets but mainly from old fishing nets collected from around the world. Discarded fishing nets are a big problem so we are partnering with some non-governmental organisations, cleaning the beaches in the Philippines, India and Africa, gathering those fishing nets and turning them into carpets. We collaborate with our nylon suppliers to take these materials, fishing nets etc, recycle them and then we buy back the recycled material."

Similarly, their most recent launch, a bio-based nylon for carpet is a real technical breakthrough with facts to back it up.

"We are using a new type of nylon where 63% comes from castor oil. Castor oil is a growing crop in India and only needs water 1 day out of 25. It also helps soil stabilisation in areas prone to erosion. It is a source of income for rural farmers and it grows in land of poor quality so it is not competing with food."

Having only just launched the bio-carpet, 'time will tell whether it is successful or not'. What is clear is that Interface is open to exploring innovative ideas and perhaps sometimes failing when trying to achieve 'Mission Zero'.

"We have tried numerous things and maybe 80% of those have failed. Both the successes and the failures in terms of

Photograph by Nick Hill, The Zoological Society of London, courtesy of Interface

innovation have been a crucial part of the story. We never close the shop to the failures; it is part of the learning. For example, we failed on things such as the leasing. The customers don't want it; the business model just doesn't work. We wanted to do this in the early stages, about 10 years ago but we didn't manage to succeed with that. We had hoped that it would extend the life of carpets but it didn't work."

Interface took this opportunity to find another solution; they started to use tiles that could replace the parts of the carpet floor that were most trodden on and degraded. Their innovation is driven by a dedication to succeed and they actively encourage employees to explore areas that they feel passionate about.

"We have overall ambitions but we don't set targets in the company. We simply say, 'we have to get to zero by 2020, come up with

radical ways to get to zero. Bring your passion. You do something and we will reward you with glory and PR'. We don't pay employees on achieving particular targets, the way we pay them is much more fundamental, by profile.

"So for instance, we had one guy who came up with a really innovative transport strategy, shifting from road to rail. Now, he is the guru of green transport in Holland because we put our PR agencies behind him and he is giving speeches here there and everywhere. That is how we reward people. Other employees learn that by doing something significant there is a lot to gain.

"When people wake up, they want to do something that has an impact on the world and have a feeling that we are working for a company in which we can do something big. We don't patronise them by telling

Courtesy of Interface

them to switch off the lights or recycle more. We ask them to work within their own sphere of influence at work. If you are the finance guy, do something related to the company cards, or if you are an engineer do something related to the factory. They come up with a project and bring it to us and then, if needed, we support them technically, financially etc.

"Rather than a top-down sustainability approach that is established in conversation with major stakeholders and then deployed as targets, we just say, 'look at where you have the biggest opportunity in your work and do something that you can be proud of in twenty years time. Interface will get to Zero, but what are you going to do, what are you going to tell your grandchildren and your friends. You have to do something that you can be proud of.' They come back with innovation that you wouldn't imagine could exist.

"Sometimes if you leave employees the space, they bring their enthusiasm and the profit comes later. Of course, sometimes profit does not come but that is part of the process of trial and error." The freedom to experiment and share ideas to accomplish the mission has meant that Interface has given itself various options throughout its history to succeed.

"We are not betting on just one. We are trying a combination of technologies and then we will see which one is sustainable in the long run.

"When we started the whole sustainable journey in 1994, we started saving waste in the factory and then we started trying to see how we could reduce the waste. The cost of raw materials is a big cost for us, it is even more than labour – so early success with the waste and therefore the cost, made the whole initiative grow bigger."

When planning for the future, the business has also given great consideration to what happens at the end of a carpet's life cycle and realises that: *"From an environmental point of view, post-consumer recycling is the best thing, as bio-based products may be shown to have very low impact. We can take old carpet and we have a machine that separates the yarn and the backing so that we can recycle each part separately.*

"We don't do a huge amount of recycling in Europe yet; it is working better in America. Not all of our customers give the carpets back yet. We need a combination of a really good piece of legislation that bans the landfill of carpet, so they have to give it back and then we need to perfect the technical processes before we can scale that up."

The extraordinary ambition to reach 'Mission Zero' that Anderson inspired his business with is evident. He 'was always there, reminding and leading by example' and has left a clear legacy with a goal for Interface to reach in the next decade.

Courtesy of Interface

Elegance

Pleasing through economy
Designing with emphathy
Demonstrating poise
Inviting interpretation

Pleasing through economy

There's a strange egg in Sant Antoni. It's bigger than any other egg you're ever likely to see and inside it is a model of Christopher Columbus' ship, the Santa Maria. The egg is a monument to Columbus, who locals claim to be a son of the Ibizan city and refers to a story about Columbus told by Italian historian Girolamo Benzoni in his 1565 *History of the New World*:

> Columbus was dining with many Spanish nobles when one of them said: "Sir Christopher, even if your lordship had not discovered the Indies, there would have been, here in Spain which is a country abundant with great men knowledgeable in cosmography and literature, one who would have started a similar adventure with the same result." Columbus did not respond to these words but asked for a whole egg to be brought to him. He placed it on the table and said: "My lords, I will lay a wager with any of you that you are unable to make this egg stand on its end like I will do without any kind of help or aid." They all tried without success and when the egg returned to Columbus, he tapped it gently on the table breaking it slightly and, with this, the egg stood on its end. All those present were confounded and understood what he meant: that once the feat has been done, anyone knows how to do it.[42]

Whether this exchange actually happened is as debatable as Columbus' Ibizan heritage, but there's a clear truth behind the story: elegant solutions to seemingly complex problems are often obvious only once they have been revealed. Hindsight brings out the genius in all of us. Prior to the invention of the paper clip in 1899, people used lengths of ribbon to hold together loose sheets of paper. Before Walter Deubner patented the world's first shopping bag in 1912, people were limited to purchasing what they (or their servants) could conveniently carry. The doorknob didn't exist until 1878. As Sherlock Holmes observed, "The world is full of obvious things which nobody by

any chance ever observes".[43] There's a fine line between "obvious" and "sublime". But then again, there's also a fine line between "obvious" and "stupid", as the double-ended toothpaste tube, wallet razor and suitcase scooter demonstrate. Business should be as pleasurably simple as Columbus' egg.

The invention of the paperclip, shopping bag and doorknob demonstrate business' ability to create more efficient, streamlined and economical solutions to life's problems. These examples are easy to appreciate but impossible to anticipate. Like Columbus' egg, they only appear obvious in retrospect. They are the result of a creative approach to problem-solving, rather than an application of workmanlike logic. They reveal that sublime solutions to problems have an artistic quality: they demonstrate sophistication, sensitivity and imagination. Economy is about more than minimising the amount of time and money spent on dirty, difficult or dangerous tasks. It is a desirable quality for a business to strive for. An opportunity to make life satisfyingly simple. An opportunity to demonstrate connoisseurship in the creation and selection of strategies for improving how the world works.

...sublime solutions to problems have an artistic quality: they demonstrate sophistication, sensitivity and imagination.

If all of this sounds idealistic and difficult to put into practice, that's because it is. Application of logic and scientific method produces a more reliable way to achieve economy. But logic and science can only be applied in a limited number of instances: where imperfect processes and rules are the root cause of inefficiency. Issues involving culture, vision, entrepreneurialism, innovation, leadership, creativity and motivation can't be fixed with science and logic. Processes and rules are blunt instruments and ill-suited to such complex challenges. But even if we appreciate the limits of logic, we remain reluctant to trust in creativity to solve the serious problems of business. We want to eat the cake of creativity without losing any of the comfort of logic. Business has attempted to capture the best of both worlds by harnessing the power of creativity through a more formal process: a process we've come to know as "design thinking".

The idea behind design thinking is extremely seductive: a process that can be relied upon to deliver creativity. This process seeks to strip out the undesirable aspects of creativity — failure, unpredictability, messiness, conflict and circularity — while still embracing the positive values, behaviours and outcomes that creativity is capable of producing. Design thinking borrows tools of creativity — insight, framing, facilitation, visualisation and prototyping – without requiring participants to get too touchy-feely. GE and P&G have been enthusiastic proponents of design thinking, emphasising the benefits that a greater focus on design has created for their innovation pipeline and their bottom line. But there is a growing sense that while design thinking has certainly benefitted organizations by providing them with a new set of processes – or crayons – with which to innovate and problem-solve, it has fallen far short of its intended purpose: to make business more creative.

Early advocates of design thinking, such as Bruce Nussbaum, have moved on. Design thinking has added a useful set of tools to innovators' toolboxes, but it has also encouraged a view that design and creativity are a thought process (as opposed to, say, a creative process). In reducing creativity to a replicable box of tricks, in ridding it of its inherent emotionality and messiness, design thinking represents a pseudo-creative process far removed from the approach most designers use to solve problems. It's difficult to imagine that design thinking would have caught on at places like GE and P&G had it been called "design feeling". As the saying goes, "a fool with a tool is still a fool". We can't rely on a process – even an innovative process – to create pleasurably simple ideas.

Creativity is not something we can wrap up in a simple process without robbing it of its magic and might. An organization's ability to solve problems and to develop elegant solutions is more likely to be limited by cultural shortcomings, rather than a lack of process. As such, creativity has to be fostered and learned, rather than mandated or prescribed. Seen this way, business becomes as much an art as a science.

People in business seem increasingly fond of describing themselves in artistic terms. Jim Stengel recently coined the term 'business artists' to describe leaders with the ability to imbue organizations with a sense of purpose. Even Warren Buffett – frequently presented as a passionate advocate of scientific methods – has declared, "I am not a businessman, I am an artist."[44] It's easy to be dismissive of these examples. For the most part, business' relationship with art is limited to patronage. BP was the "premier partner" of London's 2012 Cultural Olympiad. Deutsche Boerse sponsors an annual photography prize.

The alternative investment management business, Man, is probably best known for its sponsorship of the Booker Prize. The two worlds remain largely separate: mutually respectful at best; mutually antipathetic at worst. But the art world has plenty left to teach the world of business. As Nancy Adler pointed out, "Artists view business people as Philistines, and they in turn think of artists as a bit flaky. But if you look at the two sides objectively you will realize that creating a great work or creating a great business call for very similar qualities."[45]

These qualities were vividly described by Elliot Eisner, professor of Art and Education at Stanford University School of Education. In a 2002 lecture, Eisner defined artists as "Individuals who have developed the ideas, the sensibilities, the skills, and the imagination to create work that is well proportioned, skilfully executed, and imaginative, regardless of the domain in which the individual works."[46] Eisner believes that certain aspects of our intelligence are artistically rooted. His conclusion is that the arts have a significant contribution to make in cultivating our ability to make intelligent decisions – even in a business context.

Creativity is not something we can wrap up in a simple process without robbing it of its magic and might.

The arts encourage us to see the world from multiple perspectives. They teach us that problems can have more than one solution. They encourage us to make qualitative judgments in the absence of rules. They require us to create maximum impact with a limited set of materials. They prepare us to improvise when complex problems change with circumstance and opportunity. They demonstrate that neither words nor numbers alone can adequately explain everything we know. The arts deal in subtlety and show that small differences can have large effects. They encourage us to develop our poetic capacity and they unleash our ability to inspire as well as describe.

These are the qualities that make business sublime. They cannot be enforced through process, but they can be learnt. The Rotman School of Management in Toronto has redesigned its MBA program to more closely align the teaching of business with the liberal arts. The Stanford Graduate School of Business has also dramatically updated its approach to teaching, moving away from analytical, theoretical models and towards practical, complex problem-solving. At Harvard Medical School, students use art classes to improve their diagnostic and communication skills. A 2008 study published in the Journal of General Internal Medicine revealed that students' ability to make accurate medical observations increased 38% following completion of an art class.[47] It seems we are beginning to appreciate the value of looking at business with an artist's eye.

A 2012 survey of CEOs in the Inc. 500 revealed that the majority of CEOs describe themselves as 'creative builders'.[48] After he dropped out of college, Steve Jobs was reportedly fond of dropping in on creative classes, including calligraphy. Jack Dorsey of Twitter and Square admires the art and athleticism of ballet dancers: "They stretch themselves beyond what's normally thought possible, doing something extremely precise that somehow looks effortless."[49]

Opower
The *smiling* face of energy

Opower was founded in 2007 by Dan Yates and Alex
Laskey as a software company that offers people
much better information about their energy use.
Distributed through utility companies, the Opower
platform makes home energy users more aware of
their usage and consequently motivates them to
reduce their energy consumption.

Photograph by Aaron Clamage, courtesy of Opower

The same could be said of creative
leaders in business. By using behavioural-
science principles, Opower's software
reveals patterns of which energy
customers may have been unaware, and
personalises the information they receive
about their energy use so that it is highly
relevant (and engaging). Reports can
compare usage with neighbours and offer

energy-saving tips, with a web portal,
email and mobile alerts, and a WiFi
thermostat providing more detailed
analysis and further information.

Dan and Alex were featured in Fortune
magazine's '40 under 40' list in 2011, and in
2010 Barack Obama visited Opower's home
office, commending them on their rapid

Photograph by Aaron Clamage, courtesy of Opower

growth and "green" job creation. The company's stated purpose is 'to engage the millions of people who are in the dark about their energy use.'

Opower's business model takes into account that both utilities and their customers are their "clients". Utilities pay for the service, but end—consumers ultimately modify their behaviour based on engagement with Opower's products.

We spoke to Jeremy Faro, Senior Director of Brand, based in Opower's Washington DC headquarters.

"We're not the sort of company that is waiting for innovations to come out 10 to 15 years from now to help us save energy. We were founded because we recognise the environmental degradation going on around the world as a result of our appetite for energy, and because of our inefficient use of it. We have a software platform that is saving a tremendous

amount of energy right now by motivating people to change their behaviour.
"Everywhere we are deployed, people with access to Opower's platform from their utility are using between 2% and 3% less power just because of what we are doing: that's very motivating to everyone who works at Opower, and it's motivating to our clients too – everyone likes to feel good about what they are doing at work."

"We do this by giving everyone the information, motivation, and control that they need to save energy right now. Our entire business is based upon uncommon transparency: we take data that's yours (available through your utility) and show you how to read it, understand it, and use it. We are transforming information that's already available into something people can use – nothing could be more transparent than that. It's the very nature of the entire business: we invest heavily in information design – we have great interaction designers and user experience specialists, who design

Photograph by Aaron Clamage, courtesy of Opower

and test everything we do with all sorts of people everywhere, so that all of this great information and advice is relevant to everyone, regardless of age, income level, or access to technology. Everyone can use power more efficiently because of what we offer. In competitive markets — where you get to choose who delivers your energy to you and who you pay for your utility bills — we are seeing that people exhibit greater goodwill and favourability towards energy companies that provide them with this type of information. They understand that the utility is trying to help them have more control of their usage, and ultimately to help them manage their household expenses better. Rather than a utility being merely a public monopoly or private moneymaking entity, it's a partner helping you to run your household better than before."

Today, Opower works with more than 75 utilities in 6 countries around the world. It reaches more than 15 million people, many of whom don't even have Smart

Metres installed. *"By being friendly, engaging, clear, and honest, we set ourselves apart from our competitors. No one else sounds or looks like us. We have a brand that's appealing to utility clients as well as the larger industry, press, and investment community because we embody qualities with which most people want to share space with. The utility sector never went through the personalisation and customisation revolution that other industries in the US and UK have. Banking and telecoms went through this revolution 10 to 15 years ago.*

"Our products are much more engaging than energy customers are used to — people just haven't ever had emotional relationships with their utilities before. Our new mobile app and thermostat are our new major channels; you will be able to control and understand how your house is using energy — and how that compares to similar homes around you — from anywhere using your smart phone.

Pleasing through economy | Opower

By signing up for alerts and reminders, you'll be able to have your house warmed to your preferred temperature when you get home from a business trip or vacation, all from your smartphone — allowing it to run on efficient settings in your absence with no discomfort to you. Others are bringing out software with this type of control, but they don't have our critical behavioural component, which is what makes all the difference.

Internal culture plays a huge part in the Opower's success: *"We get to work every day with smart, talented, upbeat people: the concentration of motivated, talented staff is very high, level of employee satisfaction is very high in response to that. People are given responsibilities, and allowed to figure out how best to do things, without being micromanaged. We also have a flexible working environment, many remote employees who use technology that allows them to work effectively from their homes or small offices; we don't all have to be chained to desks all the time, and this obviously makes people happy.*

For a small company growing fast in multiple locations, it can be difficult to solidify a culture and communicate company traditions; we're not the sort of company that has a standard annual picnic, but we find other ways to come together. We hire primarily through referrals from people already working at Opower, and yet maintain a very high level of quality, which speaks volumes about the enthusiasm there is for the company."

As President Obama said during his visit: "...We need to replicate the success of clean energy companies like Opower. We need to invest in the jobs of the future and in the industries of the future, because the country that leads in clean energy and energy efficiency today, I'm absolutely convinced, is going to lead the global economy tomorrow ... I want companies like Opower to be expanding and thriving all across America. It's good for consumers. It's good for our economy. It's good for our environment."[50]

Quite an endorsement, and with plans for further expansion around the world, it's well founded.

Designing with empathy

It's difficult to argue that London is the most elegant city in the world. The weather is terrible. The people who live there aren't particularly friendly. The city lacks the charm of Amsterdam, the broad avenues of Paris and the dizzying scale of New York. But in one respect, London has served as the template for modern urban living: it is the first city to benefit from an underground passenger-carrying train system and the first city to assert itself through an integrated visual identity.

The Metropolitan Railway opened in 1863 and its success provided the stimulus for seventy years of frenzied growth. By 1924, London was overrun with over 160 independent companies running a complex network of buses, trains and trams. Each company had a distinct name, rolling stock and livery. The result was a mess. After the end of World War I, a parliamentary select committee recommended the establishment of a single traffic authority to eliminate "acute and wasteful competition", poor service and high fares. London Transport was duly set up and Frank Pick was its first Managing Director. Pick was a marketing man with a clear philosophy on design:[51]

> The test of the goodness of a thing is its fitness for use. If it fails on this first test, no amount of ornamentation or finish will make it any better; it will only make it more expensive, more foolish.

Pick is credited with integrating the new transport system within a single, consistent visual framework. Each challenge he faced in integrating London's transport system into a coherent system capable of servicing the needs of a rapidly expanding city was solved with a combination of common sense and good design. He introduced the Johnston Sans typeface in 1916 to improve legibility for passengers hurrying along crowded platforms and streets. He adopted a revised version of the now iconic London Underground roundel to signal where buses should stop.

He commissioned Harry Beck, an engineering draughtsman, to create a map capable of helping passengers navigate the rapidly expanding network. Basing his map on an electrical circuit, Beck represented each line in a different colour and simplified the course of each route into the form of a vertical, horizontal or diagonal. This style of map has since been adopted the world over, from New York to Stockholm and Sydney.

Pick also understood that art was a potent tool for creating growth. He recognised that stimulating interest in London's attractions would drive passengers to use his network with greater frequency. He commissioned renowned artists to produce a visually coherent set of posters that would inform and inspire Londoners to travel more around London. His posters also sold a dream to the city's burgeoning middle classes: an aspirational vision of suburban life. The Underground railways had expanded rapidly into rural areas and depended on populating the suburbs to create profit for these new routes. Pick used every tool available to create a compelling, coherent experience for his passengers, from selecting the textiles used to cover seats to commissioning Charles Holden's landmark station architecture. He made the following concluding statement in an address to the Royal Society of Arts in December 1935:[52]

> Underneath all the commercial activities of the Board, underneath all its engineering and operation, there is the revelation and realisation of something which is in the nature of a work of art… it is, in fact, a conception of a metropolis as a centre of life, of civilisation, more intense, more eager, more vitalising than has ever so far obtained.

Ostensibly, Frank Pick's major challenges in uniting London's transport network concerned engineering and organization. But he met these challenges with an artist's mind and eye. The elegance of his approach has left an indelible mark on the city and our experience of it.

> Harold Hotelling was not an artist. He was a statistician and economist. In 1929 he wrote an article called "Stability in Competition", which sought to explain why competing businesses have a tendency to inflict "excessive similarity" on their customers. He wanted to explain why so many businesses seem so willing to be so boring.

In his article, Hotelling invites his readers to imagine a village where people live in uniform distribution along a main street. Let's say the street is a kilometre long. He then asks us to consider what would happen if two street vendors (let's say hot dog vendors) entered into competition on the street. How would they best compete with one another? The answer depends on whether you are a vendor or a resident in the street. From the resident's perspective, the hot dog stands should be situated a quarter of a kilometre from each end.

This way, the furthest any resident will need to walk to fetch a hotdog is a quarter of a kilometre (for those unfortunate enough to live either in the middle or at each end of the street). But this won't happen. Because each vendor knows that shifting his hot dog stand closer to his competitor will move him closer to customers living in the middle of the village without sacrificing those who live at the end of the village. Over time, the hot dog vendors will gradually creep towards each other, until they meet in the middle of the village. Great news for people who live in the centre of the village. Terrible news for the people on the outskirts.

Hotelling's law — also known as the principle of minimum differentiation — describes this general tendency for businesses to bunch close together. The law explains why cities around the world contain specific shopping districts, such as Bond Street, Ginza and Fifth Avenue. Beyond location, Hotelling's law can be applied to the other ways businesses compete with one another: for example, pricing, product quality and product design. It explains why smartphones and tablets tend to look identical, why politicians compete to occupy the middle ground and – importantly for Hotelling – why cider is "too homogenous".[53]

We are surrounded by excessive sameness. For many businesses, the gravity of the average is too powerful to resist. There are lots of other businesses there. Some of them are successful. It feels safe. Many businesses avoid positioning themselves at extremes because they believe this is a niche or limiting strategy. Banks and insurers are blue. Internet start-ups are called zippy, zappy names like zopa, zappos and zoopla. Cars no longer come with fins.

Try to go around the middle: go above or below. People who are massively insecure want to be in the middle. It makes them feel safe.

There is a tendency towards the average. Hotelling's law demonstrates that this tendency isn't the result of conservative buyers. It is a consequence of undue pragmatism, diffidence and lack of imagination on the part of businesses.

But not everybody is so fond of the middle ground. In a recent interview with the *Financial Times*, the architect Peter Marino offered the following advice to aspiring architects: "Try to go around the middle: go above or below. People who are massively insecure want to be in the middle. It makes them feel safe. It doesn't make me feel safe. I can't breathe."[54] There are plenty of reasons to believe that Peter Marino knows what he's talking about: they include the boutiques he has designed for Ermenegildo Zegna, Céline, Chanel, Louis Vuitton, Christian Dior, Hublot and Lancôme, as well as countless casinos, yacht clubs, hotels, chalets, residences and spas. In 2011 alone Marino's firm completed 100 projects, all of which had budgets in excess of US$5 million.[55] None of his work could be accused of retreating towards safety. He has adorned his buildings with Murakami monsters, leather curtains, LED-embedded glass and dazzling grids of light. Marino is famously claustrophobic, which goes some way to explaining his attitude to business: if you can't join them, beat them.

The middle of a market is not as safe as it first appears. Animals that herd tend to sit at the bottom of the food chain. Excessive sameness makes companies and their products easier to confuse, easier to substitute and easier to abandon when something more interesting comes along. Before Apple introduced the iMac to the world in 1998, rival manufacturers had been content to sell computers as functional machines, encased in dull grey boxes, running the same operating system. Their excessive sameness only became obvious once a more interesting alternative became available. Computers had become a fundamental part of modern life. They were in our offices. They were in our schools. They were in our homes.

With the benefit of hindsight, it was only a matter of time before a computer manufacturer would realize that the personal computer should be as carefully and beautifully designed as the offices and homes it occupies. A century earlier, Guglielmo Marconi had invented the radio. Early radio sets were not pretty machines: plain wooden boxes from which a profusion of valves, dials and switches emanated. But within 30 years radiograms had become a central fixture of the modern home and were styled in polished wood to blend in with the furniture of the time. By the 1960s radiograms had evolved into a new form: designers such as Dieter Rams introduced clean lines, Perspex lids and a new sense of proportion. In retrospect, computer manufacturers should have known better. They had witnessed the radio evolve over a hundred years to become an object of desire.

The proliferation of "grey box" computers in the 1990s was not evidence of a lack of taste on the part of buyers, but of a lack of empathy on the part of manufacturers. The grey boxes were designed to be nonspecific, to appeal to as many people as possible. But in the end, their sole accomplishment was to be equally unappealing to everybody. They were inoffensive at best. The iMac wasn't everybody's cup of tea, but it demonstrated the importance of empathy and the danger of orthodoxy.

None of this should have been news to anybody by 1998. Almost thirty years earlier, in 1969, Saul Bass created a video for the American Bell Telephone Company (now AT&T). In the video, Bass remarked on the danger of playing it safe and on the importance of design in establishing Bell as an empathetic, eager participant in modern life:

> Many of us here today remember when [life] was quite different. The pursuit of happiness had ground to a halt. Survival was the goal. Not just to have a job, but to have a job with security. That was the prize in 1933. How long a product lasted was more important than how well it looked. Wall Street had forgotten "blue sky" and was now talking "blue chip".

> Down to earth.

> Safe was the place to be.

Customers were marvelling at the new technology. Ready to forgive imperfections... The telephone was still a marvel. The long-distance call an adventure. How did the Bell Company look then? We matched the styles, fitted the needs of the time.

We looked safe.

Durable.

Contemporary.

Part of the vacuum tube age.

Times have changed. Looks have changed. Has ours? Not enough. We still look as though we are responding to the needs of the past. When young people are looking for challenge in their careers, we seem to offer only security. When customers have come to expect technological perfection, we show up looking non-technological. In a fast-moving, competitive society, we look set in our ways. Am I exaggerating? Maybe. Just a little. Not much... Where's the look that connects us to today? Where are the visual signals that identify us as a pace-setting organisation? Is this the world's most advanced communications organisation? Or the motor pool of the quartermaster corps? How a thing looks today is as important as how it works. As never before, people are influenced by what they see. It's not just looking cleaner, or nicer, or more tasteful. It's looking a part of the society in which we operate. Advanced. We must respond to new needs.[56]

Without the aesthetic, design is either the humdrum repetition of familiar clichés or a wild scramble for novelty.

Bass' response to these new needs was to introduce a design system that gave the Bell a "new ring". The company's new approach to design was introduced in conjunction with a new promise: "we hear you". Within a year of its launch, more Americans were able to recognise Bell's new design than were able to recall the name of the President.[57] As Bass pointed out, this design was more than a cosmetic improvement: it fundamentally improved the quality of customers' experience of the company. Public telephones were easier to see from a distance. Engineers were easier to identify. Virginia Postrel defined aesthetics as "the way we communicate through the senses".[58] As such, aesthetics have an enormous impact on our experience of a business.

Apple's success is founded on this appreciation of the power of aesthetics. It didn't create the first computer. It didn't create the first phone. It didn't create the first mp3 player. Nor did it create the first tablet. But in each case it introduced an aesthetic quality that dramatically improved our ability to interact with these devices.

If you can't join them, beat them.

The aesthetics of a computer, a soft drink, a toaster or a toothbrush are fundamental to the pleasure we derive from their use. Businesses that design their products, services and environments with careful thought demonstrate an empathy that sets them apart from everybody else. In the words of Paul Rand: Without the aesthetic, design is either the humdrum repetition of familiar clichés or a wild scramble for novelty. Without the aesthetic, the computer is but a mindless speed machine, producing effects without substance. Form without relevant content, or content without meaningful form.[59]

Aesthetics isn't about providing superficial decoration for a business. It's about creating emotional meaning and substance. A keen sense of empathy helps a business navigate between the extremes of dehumanizing austerity and glitzy corporate kitsch. Even large companies can be empathetic in the way they approach design. Haier started life in 1984 when Zhang Ruimin took over a lossmaking refrigerator factory in Qingdao. One of his first actions as company CEO was to smash defective models on the factory floor with a sledgehammer to underscore his commitment to producing a quality product. Haier is now the world's leading appliance manufacturer by sales volume and 26% of its US$23 billion global revenues come from markets outside China.[60] But Zhang's turnaround of the company has not been based on quality improvement alone. The company's success is largely a result of its empathetic approach to product design.

Rather than trying to design products for a notional "global consumer", Zhang decided in 2005 that the company would customize products according to the needs of specific markets and customer types. Haier now has ten research and development centres around the world, generating nuanced design details that reflect an intimate understanding of how people want to interact with its products. These include freezers with multiple compartments for fastidious Japanese households, extra-large-capacity washers that can accommodate Middle Eastern robes, silent timer-equipped washers for Italians who want to take advantage of lower night-time energy prices, and a fridge with a giant pizza drawer for the US market.

Even in its home market, Haier has gone to extreme lengths to accommodate the idiosyncrasies of its customer base. A 2010 Forbes article tells the story of a rural farmer who complained to Haier that his washing machine had become clogged with dirt. Haier discovered that in addition to clothing, the man had been using the machine to wash the dirt from his potato harvest. Rather than pointing out the customer's folly, Haier subsequently released a washing machine designed to handle both clothes and dirty potatoes. By drawing on such idiosyncrasies, Haier has avoided falling into the trap of designing for the middle and created a meaningful and unique experience for its customers.

Designing with empathy | Zetter

Zetter
What would Wilhelmina do?

Wilhelmina, the patron of the Zetter Townhouse in London, is a difficult person to find. Her portrait hangs by the entrance to her hotel, but she is never there herself. She has influenced every aspect of the hotel's design, but none of the staff has ever met her in person. She has inspired the hotel's signature cocktails, but has yet to taste a single one.

Courtesy of Zetter

There's a simple and unexpected reason for such a hands-off approach to hospitality: Wilhelmina is a fictional character, born out of the collective imagination of co-founders Mark Sainsbury and Michael Benyan.

Sainsbury and Benyan also own the Townhouse's (big) sister hotel, the Zetter

Hotel, which is among the world's '50 Coolest Hotels' according to *Condé Nast Traveller*. But as Mark Sainsbury explains to us in the cosy warmth of the Townhouse's drawing room, the purpose of is not merely to achieve cool status. In fact, 'cool' is not an idea that Mark Sainsbury seems to feel very at home with. When they opened the Zetter Hotel in 2004, the owners' ambition was to create an accessible experience that combined good value with high design.

"If you wanted to spend less than £200 a night you would stay in the chain hotels with no character, in cookie-cutter rooms with all the drabness of international hotels. Or you stayed in the St Martins Lane Hotel [designed by Philippe Starck for Ian Schrager]. I think the Sanderson was just about to open and you paid through the nose for that experience and at the same time were made to feel like you were slightly uncool if you weren't dressed in the right clothes. We stayed in the Royalton in New York, which I loved in so many ways, but I remember that feeling when I walked past the doorman and he was better looking, taller and better dressed. I remember feeling that I was not quite making the grade in a way and feeling slightly uncomfortable. And so we loved this idea of value, design and approachability. So not too cool."

So what does a 'not too cool' hotel look like? Ian Schrager's nightclubs and hotels have defined cool for generations. They are sexy, sharp and polished. But excessive coolness comes at the expense of warmth and welcome, both cornerstones of Zetter's approach to hospitality.

"Around the same time, a week before I got married, my sister sent my fiancée and me to Babington House. It was eye opening in as much as I'd never stayed in a hotel by somebody of my generation with the relaxed approach that was lacking at the Royalton and, for me, that was on the money. Until that point hotels felt like places that you very rarely feel comfortable in. These were all contributing factors to our approach, the love of hospitality, the sense that there was this gap in the market and this discomfort with what was there."

The Zetter hotels exist to prove a point: that high design does not have to mean high prices. But they also demonstrate the difference between having high standards and high standardisation. The aim is not to build a 'global brand', but to introduce a singular love of hospitality into an idiosyncratic, eccentric set of environments. No hotel and no room is alike.

"We wanted a different feel between the sister hotels because they belong to a different period: Victorian warehouse and Georgian townhouse. We always wanted them to be different. In fact we really enjoy the idea of difference. In our DNA we're wary of 'chains' and this idea of a cookie-cutter approach to hotels. We are terrified

of being pigeonholed, as we grow with more restaurants and hotels. So the idea of doing something completely different was really appealing and obvious to us. You can share values and the attitudes towards your customer without requiring the same look. The common threads are that we don't mind taking a few risks, being a bit edgy and breaking a few rules. There is not a common aesthetic – it is all very different."

While the hotels in the group may not share a common aesthetic, each property has a distinct personality. This sounds easy in theory but is extremely difficult in practice. It's easy to dismiss hotel chains as excessively samey, but there is undeniable comfort in knowing what to expect, regardless of the city or country you may find yourself in. For many people, chain hotels are beacons of familiarity in far-flung cities: sanctuaries in the midst of strange surroundings. There's a benefit to being predictable: visitors know what to expect when they make a reservation. Excessive difference is arguably as detrimental as excessive sameness to our experience of a hotel.

Designing with empathy | Zetter

Few of us like to feel like check-in is a game of Russian roulette. To some extent, we want to be reassured that our next experience of a hotel will resemble our last: otherwise, what reason would we have to return? The Zetter hotels have successfully avoided both extremes by designing each hotel's experience with a specific person in mind. That person is not (as one might suspect) a notional 'average' customer. Nor are the hotels designed to reflect the tastes of Mark Sainsbury and Michael Benyan. Although

back over the design process it is extraordinary how often we would refer to her. What would she do? How would she play it? She was brilliantly useful in terms of being consistent and coherent."

Wilhelmina isn't the only fictional character that exists in the group. The group is building a new Townhouse in Seymour Street, under the watchful eye of Uncle Seymour.

"Uncle Seymour is going to be a little more

Courtesy of Zetter

she may be fictional, Wilhelmina plays a central role in making sure Zetter's Townhouse has a personality that is internally coherent as well as being distinct from its sister hotel.

"This place was conceived around this fictional character Wilhelmina. It started as a bit of a joke, but over time and looking

masculine. A little more austere. There are going to be greys and marbles. Although Seymour is conceived in the same way, it is going to have a very distinct and different aesthetic and personality. That is what we are after. Whatever we do, we don't want to play it safe. We don't design by committee. It is one of our great fears, as well as trying to please everybody all the time. Attention to detail, bags of personality and great staff are the compliments that I most cherish when we get feedback."

Under the watchful gazes of Wilhelmina and Seymour, the Zetter empire is steadily expanding. But Mark Sainsbury is clear that one detail in particular will always be a part of the DNA, regardless of which member of his fictional family is in charge.

"I'm massively keen on the smallest detail, no detail too small. This includes incredible caring for our staff and making sure that they are happy because it all comes from them. I think there is a sense of honesty about the place. It's a weird thing that you don't find this more often in the hospitality world, particularly in restaurants. I was incredibly lucky with the first job I had in a restaurant. I worked in this really sweet restaurant called the Union Café and I think the owners had been treated horribly when they were working for somebody else. They turned that on its head and would take us on holiday to Mallorca, give us massages and buy us mountain bikes for our birthdays. It was extraordinary and from that day on it was very obvious that we had to do something similar. So we go that extra mile. It is more difficult when you have over 100 staff here but we still have that respect for honesty towards our staff and showing it in different ways – from the parties we throw to the summer trips that we take and the massages that we give. It comes back to you. Our reasons behind it are warm, but I think you could justify it entirely financially because the return you get is people who really love their job."

This goodwill isn't limited to the hospitality extended to customers or perks offered to employees. The business' owners have a heartfelt commitment to sustainable business practices, from the partners they work with to the communities that play host to their properties. Mark Sainsbury is

a co-founder of the Sustainable Restaurant Association and frequently meets with a community of restaurateurs to share information and encouragement.

"The local surrounding area has changed a lot. It's nice to have played a role in that. There is a responsibility in that. I'm sure as we grow we could do a little bit more and give a little more back. We've organised summer festivals and markets and we've worked with community groups. I think this is a key thing."

It's evident that both owners draw significant satisfaction from the way they do business. Every ounce of effort that they put in contributes to a sense of pride that profit alone cannot deliver.

"On a personal level, there are easier ways to make money rather than sinking it into a hotel. Although we are doing very well, money is not my main motivation. Success is important but success at the expense of people's happiness is hollow to me and pretty valueless. The way you conduct yourself as a business is most important. I think that has come from my upbringing. It's amazing when you hear the feedback people give when you are human about your business."

Courtesy of Zetter

Demonstrating poise

Here's one thing we can say about crowds: it's much easier to get things done when lots of other people are with you. Being part of a crowd might weaken our sense of individuality, but the feeling of collective identity that replaces this also encourages a sense of power in numbers. One of the benefits of being willing to stand out from the crowd is that this allows us to exercise our own judgment. But this requires a rare level of self-confidence and a potentially unreasonable amount of conviction. Swimming against the stream is something salmon do shortly before they die. People who defy the wisdom of the crowd can be easy to caricature as antisocial, arrogant and more than a little bit mad.

But sometimes the individual is wiser than the crowd. In 1999, chess grandmaster Gary Kasparov played a game of internet chess against the world. His opponent was a group of 50,000 chess enthusiasts from over seventy-five countries, with moves decided by plurality vote. Kasparov won the game after sixty-two moves and four months of play.[61] He admitted after the game that the world team gave him a very hard time and that it was only after the fiftieth move that he began to feel optimistic about winning. On the other hand, Microsoft sponsored the game and revealed that at one stage 2.4% of world team votes were cast for a move that wasn't just a bad idea, but illegal.[62] Much of the analysis of the game has focused on the decision-making processes of the world team, accusations of vote rigging, the role of talented individuals in influencing the voting patterns of their teammates and the involvement of Microsoft itself. Kasparov, in comparison, comes across as a paragon of calm and control.

Poise is the quality of steadfastness and composure. It is typically attributed to individuals but it can also apply to companies or groups of people. Illy is one such company. Its CEO, Andrea Illy, is the grandson of founder Fancesco and custodian of one of Italy's most iconic and widely respected brands. Six million cups of Illy coffee are consumed each day in over 140 countries around the world.[63] Although Illy has grown significantly since its establishment in 1933, the company has held steadfastly to a passionate belief in excellence and building a sustainable business. This means that Illy has focused exclusively on making the best coffee possible. The company pioneered the use of laser-guided sorting machines to ensure defective beans don't find their way into its products. Unlike Starbucks, Illy has no instant product. It produces a single blend of 100% Arabica beans, meticulously combined to create the company's distinctive taste – "perfect", in the company's own words. Illy employs a team of agronomists to search for the world's best bean-producing farms: a combination of climate, soil type and a farmer willing to do what it takes to make a great product.

No amount of pressure from outside seems likely to tempt or force Illy to change its approach to business. If restaurants, cafés and bars do not meet the company's exacting standards, they aren't permitted to sell Illy products. The company insists that its coffee must be served the "Illy way", pioneered by Francesco Illy in 1933. Illy farmers are reputedly paid a premium of around 30%[64] above the market price for their coffee, in return for a commitment to adhere to the company's strict agricultural, environmental and social standards. This has put the business into direct conflict with the Fairtrade Foundation, which Illy believes creates higher prices without a commensurate increase in quality. The implication is that Fairtrade disincentivises farmers to grow quality coffee. As a result, Andrea Illy believes Fairtrade represents an unsustainable model for the coffee industry to follow.

Rather than falling in line with other people's models for coffee production, Illy has instead decided to assert the virtues of its own "bean to cup" approach in the form of the Universita del caffe di Trieste. The Udc is Illy's centre of excellence for coffee, where café and restaurant workers can learn to make coffee the "Illy way". Beyond this, Illy runs a €15,000 five-month master's degree in Coffee Economics and Science, covering agronomy, processing, marketing, supply chain management and finance. The venture's aim is not to make money, but to communicate the company's beliefs to a wider audience, as well as to connect the company to passionate, ambitious people who may one day join the company. The Udc also makes one point abundantly clear: Illy cares too much about coffee culture to trust anybody else with its preservation.

We most admire poise at times of upheaval, uncertainty or adversity. The insurance industry arguably bears the brunt of the fallout from economic, political and social turbulence. In the past decade, the industry has had to foot the bill for a string of

People who defy the wisdom of the crowd can be easy to caricature as antisocial, arrogant and more than a little bit mad.

environmental catastrophes, terrorist activity, natural disasters and economic disintegration. Insurers have suffered from a lack of public confidence, exacerbated by a liquidity crisis at AIG, which prompted the US Treasury to bail out the company in 2008. In the midst of this maelstrom, one insurer has lived up to its promise of being "as good as our word". Hiscox was founded in 1946 when Ralph Hiscox formed the Roberts & Hiscox partnership. At the heart of the company is a mission to challenge convention. Over the four years between 2007 and 2011, the company has defied a difficult environment to grow its business by over 20%, delivering an average return on equity of 17.3%. In contrast to many of its competitors, Hiscox has been careful not to rely on technology to control risk, encouraging its underwriters to exercise their own intuition and experience in making decisions.

Robert Hiscox, the company's head for the past forty-two years, has been notoriously resistant to passing fads and what he described in an interview with *The Independent* as the insurance market's "lack of integrity and appalling underwriting in the 1980s and 90s."[65] Under his leadership, Hiscox has stood out in an industry traditionally viewed as boring and uniform – a red and black beacon in a sea of blue. When customers make a claim, Hiscox's philosophy is to assume they have a valid reason for doing so. The company is determined to reiterate its steadfastness and to distance itself from the negative attention its industry has attracted:

> It's not hard to view the world as something beautiful but somehow broken.
>
> Institutions have let us down. More effort is spent on blaming others than finding solutions. And today it seems a person's word has lost its worth.
>
> Yet if the fading of these values disturbs us, then surely they must still matter?
>
> We still admire honesty, fairness, and the courage it takes to speak out against what's wrong.
>
> Whatever you choose to call it, honour is still at the heart of how most of us try to live our lives.
>
> At Hiscox, we exist to make good in times of loss. And give our word that we will be there, when you need us.
>
> If you believe that business can still be done on the strength of a handshake, and that promises are still worth keeping, then you are most definitely not alone.[66]

These are bold statements to make. Once uttered, they cannot be taken back. There is something almost maddeningly self-confident about such a level of self-possession in an industry that is constantly buffeted by misfortune and loss. Many insurers have sensibly decided to keep their heads below the parapet. But poise, steadfastness and composure can't be turned off when times get tough. Although they operate in very different areas, Illy and Hiscox share very similar qualities: a confidence born from experience that they will hold their nerve and keep their heads, even when all about them others are losing theirs.

KTC
Made in China

KTC (which stands for Knowledge, Technology and Craft) are manufacturers of quality performance clothing for several well-known brands, with factories in the Guangdong province of China and in Laos.

Courtesy of KTC

And they're on a mission to challenge the perception of what 'Made in China' means, as well as improving the conditions and treatment of their workforce. As members of the Fair Wear Foundation and Fair Labour Association, they are the exception in the sector and the region. The membership criteria for these organisations are extremely demanding – requiring full company audit reports and a degree of openness that is rare in this manufacturing world.

We talked to Gerhard Flatz, Managing Director of KTC, about the challenges of operating in the developing Chinese economy. He told us just how much KTC has changed since it was set up and explained his passion for two things – quality and people.

"The company was set up in 1971 by two Austrians, Hans Kremmel and Dieter Waibel, importing Swiss yarns to make turtlenecks for a company called Benedikt Maeser, who were predominant in the 70s and 80s for high quality ski wear. Then in 1973 we began working with Adidas, at one point becoming their exclusive sourcing partner for production out of Thailand,

Courtesy of KTC

Macau, China and Hong Kong. We then got more involved in luxury ski wear and premium functional apparel."

After joining the company in 1997, Gerhard took over as MD in 2008, when he began reconfiguring the business and started on the initiative of seriously looking into compliance and sustainability issues.

"Business is absolutely about people in our industry. What is interesting is that craft interacts automatically with this kind of compliance, sustainability and how you treat people. We did an internal satisfaction survey last year where we measured how happy the workforce is, and we noticed that, because of generational change and the one-child policy, some needs of the people have totally changed. It's much harder to get really skilful people now, I think of these younger people as the so-called lost generation, who just apply for a job because

the basic conditions are good, and we are pay well in our sector. They stay for a short time – around four weeks – and then move to another company. This is common in the manufacturing industry all over China.

"So we launched an Apprenticeship Programme in 2011, and this year 100% of the workforce in our China factory achieved the first stage – a state recognised apprenticeship. We have a beginner, an intermediate and then a master level. For me, it's important to get the younger generation behind the machines, so that when they get to nineteen, they get a state recognised certificate. We need to get real stability within the workforce, especially as craftsmen, because at the moment younger people are more interested in working in the service industry than in craft and trade. Whenever economies are developing, the manufacturing industries are the first ones to lose people."

"Being premium payers in this industry is helping us, and it's interesting that we can see that it is not a bottom line negative when you pay the highest salary. By paying more, our people are more efficient, because they are more motivated. And because of this, a lot of the talent stays longer, and the longer they stay the more efficient they get.
We definitely want to celebrate our work force more. Our five year plan is that, as salaries are increasing all over China, we want to employ 80% locals behind the machines and reduce migrant labour to 20%. This will help us move forward, because people will stay longer and there will be less fluctuation in the workforce."

Gerhard's plan is already starting to work – retaining workers is vital, and the actions taken have helped to reduce the level of people leaving for other jobs from 45% to below 20% within six months.

To underpin their commitment to quality, their workforce, and good practice, KTC has joined the Fair Wear Foundation, a non-profit organisation that works with companies and factories to improve labour conditions for garment workers.

"Before we convinced the Fair Wear Foundation to accept us, factories were not generally considered for membership because it was only open to brands, and the couple of factories that were members were attached to existing brands. We were accepted for membership in 2011, and then this year we decided to take the next step and joined the Fair Labour Association. I think in the manufacturing world we are the only company that's a member of both organisations."

A full company audit into working practices and conditions is mandatory to become a member of the Fair Wear Foundation, and shows just how much KTC is prepared to be open and transparent with their employees, customers and other suppliers and partners. The audit report[67] covers production planning, training capabilities, transparency, and other management and employer practices – and it's available online for anyone to read. Not exactly what you'd expect from a clothing manufacturer in China, given the long-standing perception of the industry.

As Gerhard says: *"I need the outside world to monitor me and tell me what I am doing wrong, because when you are running an operation daily because you get operationally blind. The media is also invited to monitor us and we have several journalists visiting us regularly. For me this is the most important thing to go forwards and to safeguard this operation is to be as transparent as possible and to get as many comments as possible to go into the next century."*

When re-configuring the business, Gerhard Flatz also had to consider the brands and partners that they supply.

"This was very important in the transformation period; when partners don't stand behind a transforming company then it is a bit of a problem. There is a potential risk in case we failed, and the brands could have chosen not to stay with us. When we started the transformation, we had forty partners, and we now have ten, because some got cold feet. The guys who remained on board, who saw that it could be beneficial for them made up the shortfall of the thirty who were gone. In the end I brought in business where I could get much larger volumes, so that I could balance out the production and longer time frames. The benefit in the end was that we had better quality output, but at the same time, we could then sell it for a lower price. Before we had the problem that we always worked with small quantities, so the work in

Demonstrating poise | KTC

Courtesy of KTC

itself was always a learning curve. I once joked that KTC is not a factory, it is the biggest sample studio on the planet. We are true design and development partners."
"Our current partners are the guys that understood the path that I was going on and were really grateful that I was doing it. It gives them a unique position in the market as they can showcase the superb quality, which helps them sell more at a higher price point. The sustainability and transparency parts are also becoming increasingly important because consumers are becoming more and more interested in it."

Gerhard intends to continue along this path, and is currently working with someone from the organic food industry, to develop KTC's own sustainability programme, adopting the practices from farming, and learning from the fact that they are even more restricted and regulated than the manufacturing industry.

"The next thing is not just taking care of people, but also to consider the chemicals used in the garments. It's the next step forward and my next big project: ultimate transparency by implementing a system demonstrating the possibilities we have, and not just relying on old established approaches."

KTC continues to work with some of the most premium brands in the world, especially in the sports sector, and Gerhard continues to campaign for a re-interpretation of what 'Made in China' means. He wants it be a badge of pride, giving performance sportswear products a feeling of the highest quality, expressing the sentiment in KTC's phrase "the art of performance manufacture".

This why KTC is different: standing fast to their principles, demonstrating poise and leading the way to a new understanding of 'Made in China' that will hopefully spread

Demonstrating poise | KTC

around the world, and not least inside China itself where, culturally, businesses shy away from showcasing success or working methods and practices.

As Gerhard says, *"There are definitely a lot of beautiful businesses in China, they just don't showcase themselves as such. They are hiding behind the cultural curtain. After all, in history, 2,500 years ago, the Chinese were the first craftsmen."*

Courtesy of KTC

Inviting interpretation

How does a business profit from elegance? The majority of this chapter has focused on the elusive nature of elegance. Creating elegance in a business context is an art form and requires us to learn to behave as artists. This can be a messy, complex, involved process and relies heavily on our willingness to think creatively and execute single-mindedly.

So why bother?

Even if the process is difficult, the result is a business that is pleasurably simple. Elegance makes companies more efficient by eliciting the maximum impact with the minimum effort. We dislike excess in principle: the term suggests waste, superfluity and overindulgence. But we have a natural tendency to fill in blanks. Strategy documents frequently run to hundreds of pages. Guidelines and manuals abound. Employee handbooks are crammed full of policies and processes. In our keenness to provide clarity of direction, we have created a climate of policy overload. According to the *British Medical Journal*, over 300 separate guidelines exist to govern the way doctors in the UK treat patients. It is impossible for any person – even a doctor – to retain this amount of information. Businesses spend a lot of time creating a lot of stuff that everybody subsequently ignores or forgets.

This is a price we are prepared to pay for the illusion of control. A manager who doesn't issue a comprehensive set of directives is open to accusations of laziness or craziness. When Ricardo Semler took over his father's engineering company in the 1980s, he decided to ditch many of the policies and processes many of us accept as an inevitable part of doing business. No official working hours. No business plan. No job descriptions. No sign-off process. He even dabbled with the idea of workers setting their own pay. His revolution aimed to eliminate the unnecessary policies and processes that were making his company inefficient, uninspiring and inflexible. Although his methods were extreme, they weren't entirely mad. Semler understood that leaders have a very limited ability to control their business. Excessive policies and auditing make managers feel more in control, but this is frequently at the expense of the people who are actually responsible for doing all of the work. These managerial comfort blankets come at a high price, both in terms of efficiency and company culture.

So is Ricardo Semler lazy, crazy or amazing? It's hard to know. He was the poster boy of a new, democratic approach to business in the 90s. According to his Wikipedia page, Semler's approach resulted in a 65% decrease in inventory, a product defect rate of less than 1% and a growth in annual revenue from US$4 million in 1982 to $212 million in 2003.[68] He was a visiting scholar at the Harvard Business School. He wrote some immensely popular books. In a recent interview, Semler reported that annual revenue growth is still as high as 40%.[69] But despite all of the interest in Semler's story, few businesses have been willing to adopt his minimalist approach to leadership. Elegance comes at a price: control. It places an enormous burden of trust on employees to interpret what a company hopes to achieve and to decide for themselves how best to contribute through their own effort and ingenuity.

There's a difficult balance to strike here. On the one hand, managers need to demonstrate to shareholders that they are diligent in setting strategy and overseeing its execution. They will be held accountable if their strategy fails to result in commercial success. On the other hand, they rely on the motivation and talent of their employees to translate strategy into action. The example set by Ricardo Semler frightens us because his approach is uncomfortably novel. But Semler's business is not the only example of a "less is more" approach to management.

Businesses spend a lot of time creating a lot of stuff that everybody subsequently ignores or forgets.

The Toyota Production System (TPS) has drawn significant interest from the business community and is widely credited with the attainment of high quality at low cost. Much of the literature on TPS focuses on specific practices, such as kanban cards and quality circles, but more in-depth studies of Toyota's success demonstrate the underlying importance of the company's culture of problem-solving. Toyota's approach bears some remarkable similarities to Semler's. A 2008 article on Toyota published in the Harvard Business Review reveals that TPS is as much about delegation of trust and responsibility to the workforce as it is about efficiency of process.[70] This goes some way to explaining why other companies have struggled to replicate TPS. In the article, the authors describe the importance of the employee to making TPS work:

> Toyota believes that efficiency alone cannot guarantee success... What's different is that the company views employees not just as pairs of hands but as knowledge workers who accumulate chie — the wisdom of experience — on the company's front lines.

Seen from the outside, Toyota appears remarkably prescriptive in its approach. Clear goals are established and work is carried out in a well-defined sequence of steps. But Toyota adopts a "broad brush" approach to setting strategy: an ambitious goal is communicated to employees, but it is left to them to solve the problem of how that goal should best be achieved. Toyota's belief is that there is only one way to promote a culture of problem-solving and that is to give people problems to solve. The article quotes Zenji Yasuda, a former Toyota senior Managing Director, who describes the importance of "painting with broad strokes":

> If he makes [the goal] more concrete, employees won't be able to exercise their full potential. The vague nature of this goal confers freedom on researchers to open new avenues of exploration; procurement to look for new and unknown suppliers who possess needed technology; and sales to consider the next steps needed to sell such products.

Toyota demonstrates that you don't have to be crazy to adopt a "laissez-faire" approach to business. Leaders who don't trust employees to interpret their strategy can only be disappointed. At best, employees will carry out tasks as prescribed. Leaders who invite their employees to interpret strategy for themselves are also open to disappointment: there's always a risk that people will let you down. But there's also a significant upside: inviting people to interpret strategy for themselves creates the possibility that people will deliver surprising, innovative approaches to their work. Nobody knows more about a role than the person who fills it. This is the essence of elegance: minimal input invites maximum impact because it invites people to bring the best of themselves to a challenge.

The same is true of how a business interacts with its customers. Many businesses seem to want to dictate their relationship with people: to educate them about the virtues of their products and services, to prescribe how they should be used and to propagate a specific image through their brand(s). Where the world of art is purposefully ambiguous and invites interpretation, business is a world of data, precision, explanation and rigour. We expect leaders to set a strategy and demonstrate rigour in directing and overseeing its execution. The aim is to leave as little room for interpretation as possible.

Companies can get quite upset when misinterpretation happens. In 2006, Frédéric Rouzaud succeeded his father Jean-Claude as Managing Director of Louis Roederer, the winery behind hip-hop's Champagne of choice, Cristal. Shortly after his appointment, Mr. Rouzaud was asked by the Economist magazine to comment on the potential damage to his brand of its adoption by the hip-hop community. His response was far from positive:

> What can we do? We can't forbid people from buying it. I'm sure Dom Pérignon or Krug would be delighted to have their business.[71]

These comments were not favourably received by rapper Jay-Z, who publicly condemned Mr. Rouzaud's views as "racist".[72]

A quick dip into the history of the brand demonstrates what a close fit Cristal is with the "bling bling" lifestyle hip-hop aspires to. Cristal was created in 1876, when Tsar Alexander II of Russia asked Louis Roederer to create a Champagne for his own personal consumption: "a unique wine in quality and bottle".[73] In other words, he wanted to make sure that his wine looked better than everybody else's, as well as tasting better. He was the Jay-Z of Tsarist Russia.

But few companies achieve success by appealing to a single (intended) group of people. Levi Strauss invented the modern concept of "blue jeans" in 1873 to clothe gold prospectors on their way to California – a far cry from the young urbanites that the company now considers its principal customer. Ray-Ban sunglasses were originally intended for the US military, not rock stars and film icons. Unintended audiences frequently appropriate products, services and brands. As Mr. Rouzaud points out above, there is little businesses can do to prevent this from happening. If companies cannot prevent interpretation, then they should learn to embrace it.

How can inviting interpretation benefit a business when most companies would prefer to choose how people think, feel and behave towards them? Because interpretation creates meaning. Businesses become more interesting and immersive when they encourage us to provide our own interpretation of them. They excite debate. They stimulate conversation. They provoke a response. Art critic Terry Barrett summed up the power of interpretation the following way:

> To interpret is to respond in thoughts and feelings and actions to what we see and experience... When we look at a work of art we think and feel, move closer to it and back from it, squint and frown, laugh or sigh or cry, blurt out something to someone or no one... When writing or telling about what we see and what we experience in the presence of an artwork, we build meaning, we do not merely report it.[74]

When a business tells people how it wants them to think, feel and behave, the best it can hope for is that they will understand the message and comply with it. But a business that invites interpretation allows people to attribute to it a deeper sense of meaning. To share stories about it. To build communities around it. To build virtual communities around it. To allow successive generations to find new meaning in the same products and services, words and pictures. To help us question our own priorities about life.

Threadless
Design in the community

Since launching in November 2000, graphic t-shirt company, Threadless now has over 2.5 million members and has received over 400,000 submissions from 12 year olds to 60 year olds.

Courtesy of Threadless

Founder, Jake Nickell describes his business that began as a hobby as: *"A community-based design company. Artists around the world submit design ideas to our design site. Our community votes on them to help us figure out which ones are the best ones and then we turn the best ones into products that we make and sell and we compensate the artists for their work.*

"It took a good two years for us to realise that it was a business, it was really just a hobby

where, I'd be keeping these Tupperware boxes of shirts in my apartment and in my lunch-breaks at work, I would take whatever orders we had had from the previous day and head down to the post-office. It was just a fun, creative thing."

Since setting up, Nickell's role has shifted from CEO of the company to focusing on the community side of the business. As Chief Community Officer, Nickell makes sure that Threadless is a great place for people to participate on a daily

Inviting interpretation | Threadless

basis. Threadless celebrates individualism within a community, where crowd sourcing has made the Threadless community essential to its success.

"Crowd sourcing is a business model that has been bastardised a bit. A lot of people are seeing it as a way to outsource their work to this crowd of people who do it for you faster, cheaper, better. That is not why we started at all. In our case it is much more like we noticed this already existing community of people doing amazing things. We are able to come in and throw gasoline on that and make it much more successful. You have all these artists who are creating stuff whether Threadless existed or not. What we are able to do is find really cool opportunities for people."

For example, the Art Director for the 2008 Obama campaign, John Slabyk, was discovered through his designs on Threadless. The manner in which Threadless draws in a worldwide crowd to contribute has meant that the designs have an active relevance to social, political and economical events. The success of Threadless has also highlighted a cultural shift that is taking place:

"When I was growing up, everybody was listening to the same music, going to the same movies, watching the same five TV stations. Now in all kinds of different industries you are seeing stuff getting spread out a lot more. People are able to be unique and find something to personally identify with. You see it in fashion where we went from department stores to small outlets to fast-fashion and e-commerce. You see it in TV with the move from network stations to cable to satellite to YouTube. And in music, the other day I was looking up the top-selling music album of all time was Michael Jackson's Bad. It came out in 1987 and in 2011, you would have had to group together the top 70 albums of the

Courtesy of Threadless

year to reach those kinds of sales. Everything has spread out into so many different niches. At Threadless, we come out with a new product every single day whereas usually fashion is seasonal. We have a huge variety of products. We are not defined by one style. There is a huge variety of people who can identify with

Threadless in ways that are personal to them."

Nickell believes that American author and journalist, Daniel Pink's 2011 book, 'Drive: The Surprising Truth About What Motivates Us' defines what Threadless is all about. Autonomy, mastery and purpose.

"Autonomy because you are on your own, you are able to design whatever you want, it is your own objective, your initiative. Mastery — you are learning a lot. For every design you make you get tonnes of feedback from our community, people commenting on it, saying what they like or don't like about it. And just by submitting over and

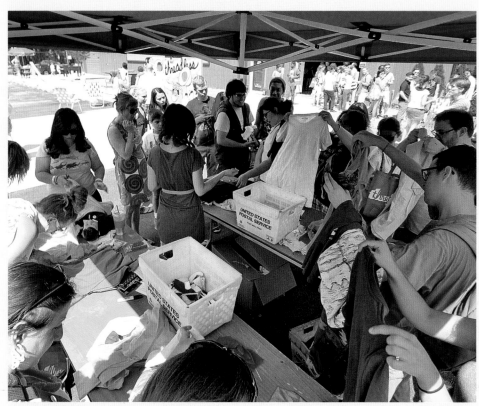

Courtesy of Threadless

over again, you are honing your skills and becoming a better illustrator. Purpose – there is this bigger community that you are contributing to, it is not just yourself, you are working with a large group of people too." The community within Threadless is generated by visitors finding common interests through the backgrounds of the designs featured on the website. This is what makes Threadless accessible and appealing to such a wide audience. Whether it is fashion or organic foods, Nickell identifies the importance of the story behind designs and products.

"Everybody wants a story. People are buying into a story, there has to be a reason behind why they are purchasing the thing they are. Usually people get sucked into Threadless through a design that they like.

We come out with a new design at least every single day, sometimes more. With all the designs that we are actually releasing, usually there is something that people can connect with."

Nickell's drive to encourage individuality and relevance stems from his time in high school: *"I was really frustrated with the fact that all the popular kids in school were always wearing just logo shirts like Abercrombie, Tommy Hilfiger, whoever it was. I didn't like how in fashion, real casual fashion, like t-shirts, the only option was to buy something with somebody else's corporate logo on them. So I always wore band shirts, because at least then you are supporting an individual. Art t-shirts never really existed that I knew of before Threadless.*

Inviting interpretation | Threadless

"Everything that we are doing every day as a business is about finding opportunities for artists, getting their work printed, getting them paid for it and making sure their name is on it, it is all about the artist. By doing that if we maintain our integrity and do a good job with that, we are creating a very prosperous business too. The business model is built into the reason we exist."

As well as helping artists grow their careers, Threadless also has partnerships with communities such as the online gaming world Minecraft and leading brands such as Disney, Cartoon Network and Gap.

"We were worried what a partnership with a big company would do to our community and customers. It actually became a Harvard case study. I went to the Harvard classes and what we ended up learning is that from the customer side, our customers hold Threadless really dear to them, almost like as secret, where they don't want everybody else to have what they have. Then on the artists' side, they want their art to be everywhere. They would love for as many people as possible to be able to buy and see what they have made. So we decided that we would not sell the same designs through these partners as those that are available on Threadless. We need to make sure that as we are expanding through these new growth opportunities such as partnerships etc, that we are not doing anything other than maintaining integrity as we grow. It is easy for a business to get larger and to focus more on optimising revenue, usually for short-term benefits. Often, the things that give a business its integrity are much more long-term thinking and brand building that you can't even quantify.

"I started with t-shirts because it was easy. Every small town has a t-shirt store. Now, we are really focused on making a lot more than just t-shirts because there are plenty talented enough to design more than just t-shirts and

they would love to see their designs on other products and distributing them in more places other than just Threadless.com. It is a huge growth opportunity for us and for our artist community."*

Threadless began as a hobby and 13 years on and Nickell continues to imbed the essence of fun, enjoyment and fondness within the business.

"Every year we have a meet-up here, where artists from all over the world are invited to hang out. The last one we had was 25th August 2012, where we had 2000 RSVPs from around the world. It is a weeklong affair, where artists come on the Tuesday and leave the next Wednesday. It all comes together on the Saturday when we have speakers, screen printing set up for t-shirts, a DIY thing for tote-bags and we had a couple of bands play. Business needs to be a positive part of your life, not just work or a job that you have to go to. It is more of a lifestyle, where you are doing the things you do everyday at work because it is something that you actually want to do with your life. It is not just a way to pay your bills. It is not something that just applies to entrepreneurs."

Craft

Connecting through stories
Applying the human hand
Developing a signature style
Creating a sense of theatre

Connecting through stories

What do stories have to do with business?
It's comforting to think of business as the realm of fact: the vocabulary of business is data; logic is its grammar. Storytelling, on the other hand, is the realm of fantasy, fiction and folklore. Stories are made up by shady marketing men in shiny suits to add a positive spin to unspectacular businesses. Stories are unconcerned with the truth. And when businesses tell such stories, they trade in bullshit. As Harry Frankfurt describes in his excellent essay "On Bullshit":[75]

> It is just this lack of connection to a concern with truth – this indifference to how things really are – that I regard as of the essence of bullshit.

Bullshit seems to pervade every aspect of modern corporate life. Even people who run businesses don't trust their own marketers not to manufacture meaningless mumbo jumbo. According to a recent study of CEOs carried out by UK consultancy Fournaise,[76] 80% of company leaders don't trust and "are not very impressed by the work done by marketers." In comparison, 90% of those polled said that they "trust and value the opinion and work of CFOs and CIOs."

It's absolutely right to view the stories companies tell with suspicion. More often than not, they really are created by marketing men, some of whom really do wear shiny suits. But we are not powerless to resist this tidal wave of corporate spin. David Lubars, Chairman and Chief Creative Officer of advertising network BBDO, famously made the observation that people are like roaches when it comes to marketing mumbo jumbo: "You spray them and spray them and they get immune after a while."[77] We are all born with lie detectors (more commonly referred to as brains) and we are frequently called upon to use them.

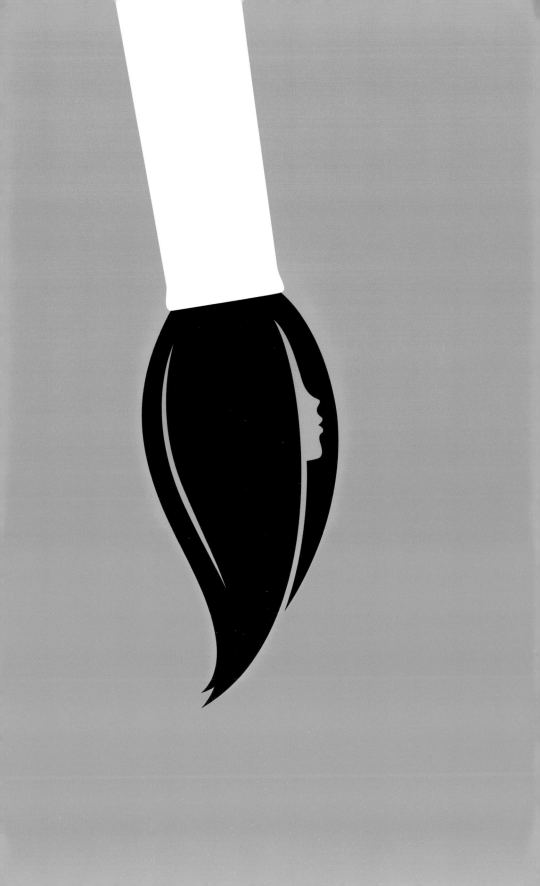

Many companies are intent on emitting clouds of hot air, with the idea that this will make them seem more important to the people they care about. We don't have to look far for examples. One of our colleagues passed a Dow Chemicals billboard on the way to work the other day, plastered with the following words: "Solutionism. The new optimism." The current edition of *Monocle* magazine features an advertisement from Hyundai informing us that "This is where brilliance happens" and exhorting us to "live brilliant". Advertising for American Eagle Outfitters encourages you to "live your life" and Hilton has legally registered the phrase "travel should take you places".

It's easy to become immune to this kind of communication. It's also easy to become immune to the more generic form of corporate speak indulged in by businesses: the type of rhetoric that involves bland statements about commitment to excellence, empowering people and customer intimacy. Front pages of annual reports are fertile sources of "play it safe" communication:

> "The best firm for our clients, our people
> and our communities."[78]
> "The way forward."[79]
> "Connecting with customers."[80]

Safe communication is as useless as no communication at all. The statements above do nothing to explain why we should care about the companies they relate to. Perhaps they are purposefully bland, designed to discourage investors from scrutinising their annual accounts. The overriding impression they leave us with is of a missed opportunity. Annual global advertising spend alone is estimated at US$506.3 billion in 2012[81] – roughly the same as Egypt's annual GDP.[82] This is an enormous amount of money to spend on this type of message.

So how can companies motivate people to care about what they do?

None of the examples above involve stories, even though storytelling is a powerful vehicle for creating meaning. It turns facts into a narrative that we can relate to. Facts provide information, but stories add interest and inspiration. Non-profit organisations are well versed in presenting data through a story. The WWF has launched a "Size of Wales" project, which aims to attract £160,000 of donations to protect an area of East African rainforest the size of Wales. In seeking donations to respond to the West Africa child hunger crisis that affects 18 million people, Save the Children tells the story of a single child – Noura – a severely undernourished eight month-old from Niger, who the charity has helped to nurse back to strength.

Effective storytelling in business is not about propagating nonsense or telling lies. It's a way of organising and simplifying information to create meaning. It's a way of establishing relevance and demonstrating that you've considered your audience. We were recently introduced to a new business called Sugru. Sugru makes a malleable self-setting rubber that can be used to repair or enhance everyday objects. According to the company's website, the product's patented technology "is unique in its combination of hand-formability, self-adhesion and flexibility when cured".[83] Apparently tens of thousands of people across seventy-six countries have used the product. So far, so boring... But the business bursts into life when its founder, Jane Ni Dhulchaointigh, tells the story of how she set up the business: "From 'hmm' to 'yay' via 'eureka' and 'wow'". Using a combination of words and pictures, she invites us to share in the highs and lows of establishing a small business. Suddenly Sugru starts to make sense. The company's homepage also contains a set of photos taken by Sugru users: a series of images of everyday objects such as frying pans, towel rails and lawnmowers, which have all been "upgraded" using Sugru. Each image is an intimate portrait of the product's ability to inspire creativity.

Courtesy of Surgu.com

Make your own prescription swimming goggles
Since I have quite a strong prescription, I'm more or less blind when I swim. I don't want to buy prescription goggles as they're so expensive, but I had several old, ordinary glasses as well as regular swimming goggles. So, I Sugru'ed them together!
The end result works really well!

Mikael

These examples demonstrate how stories about customers, employees and suppliers can create a sense of intimacy and provide tangible evidence of the good work a company does. The intimate nature of the stories above makes them easy to separate from corporate claptrap. They remind us that business is a fundamentally human enterprise. It's significant that these stories aren't generated by the business itself. In exhibiting customer stories on its website, Sugru acts as a curator, not as a creator. The product plays a prominent role in each story, but hero status is reserved for the customers themselves: it's what you do with the product that counts.

Stories can also act as a form of corporate memory, connecting businesses to their past. IBM's wild ducks featured prominently in their centenary celebration, acting as a reminder to the business of the ideals that define IBM as a business. But IBM's aptitude for storytelling extends far beyond wild duck tales. Throughout the past sixty years, IBM has employed storytelling across innovative media to convey important ideas to the world. The first of these films was created in collaboration with the Eames Office in 1958: "The Information Machine" is a narrated cartoon that describes the relationship between man, memory, information and imagination through the ages — from prehistory through to modern day, via genies, Ancient Greeks, early explorers, and Renaissance inventors. The film sought to explain the importance of the company's machines to a technically inexpert audience, by providing "creative man with a higher platform on which to stand and from which to work". Many films have followed. Rather than providing mere information, all of IBM's stories provide illumination, provoke thought and – at least in our case – prompt delight.

Stories are the vehicles through which we share knowledge and establish cultural norms. We use parables to convey moral messages. Anecdotes reveal our sense of humour. Legends inspire awe. Legitimising myths justify the dominance of specific social groups. Within a business, stories are a powerful force for creating company culture. Legend has it that Sam Walton, founder of Wal-Mart, was arrested in Brazil for crawling around a supermarket on his hands and knees measuring the width of its aisles. This tells us a tremendous amount about the culture of his business: a focus on continuous improvement, driven by an insatiable hunger for learning. Stories humanize a business. They demonstrate emotional intelligence. They communicate values and purpose. They fascinate. They draw us in. They reveal truths that information alone cannot expose.

Connecting through stories | Rapha

Rapha
Glory and suffering

Simon Mottram, founder and CEO of Rapha, has a goal — to make road cycling the most popular sport in the world.

Courtesy of Rapha

"I set up the company because the sport wasn't being celebrated, and even if I went into a bike shop (which is all about cycling) the products were terrible. They weren't talking about the sport or showing any pictures of it, if there was a race on they weren't showing it, and they weren't talking about it. They weren't asking about my riding; there were just badly designed products. The idea for the company came from that really and the catalyst was that I couldn't find anything to buy.

You have to use the world's best fabrics to make the products elegant, simple, beautiful and attractive to connect on a aesthetic level because the sport is beautiful in aesthetic, it has an amazing look and feel that I think is really attractive and that the rest of the world should recognise.

"The first Rapha collection was launched in July 2004, at a month-long Rapha exhibition of cycling memorabilia and events called 'Kings of Pain'. Since then, the Rapha product range has grown dramatically and the brand has become synonymous with the highest levels of quality, style and performance.

"I was desperately keen to find a role model — a business that was going to go direct to consumer, have direct relationships with customers, with a focus on a niche passion, but after looking long and hard I couldn't find any direct role model. Patagonia was close as it was focused on Yves Chouinard's view and his sport. But, while it did go direct it wasn't quite the same. We have a narrow perspective, the sport of road cycling. Not track, just road. But we do have a very broad range of products (probably into broader categories than Patagonia), stretching from travel to writing books, running cafes and making clothing. In the context of road cycling they all makes sense. I think the reason there aren't many directly comparable brands, is because it's really hard to develop a business across multiple categories of product and service categories, Every business in there has its own challenges. It only makes sense to do this if the idea the business is pursuing is so sharp that it is a powerful drive for everything that you do.

"In order to get investment at the beginning, I made a film using very emotional footage of racers in the 1960s – it was cheap and simple – and I put a Pavarotti aria as the sound track. I used this with potential investors, and talked a lot about potential Rapha customers, their lives, and why they like the sport, guys in their 30s, 40s, 50s sitting behind desks, yearning for a more active physical human experience that wasn't about conference calls, interviews and spread sheets. I did a lot of analysis of lots of numbers, but it was difficult to convince people about the potential of road cycling at the time and it took over 200 meetings to get enough investment to start.

"There hasn't really been a single 'breakthrough moment' in the development of Rapha but rather a series of little steps. We started out with a clear plan and there is nothing we are doing now that doesn't make total sense from the original business plan. The vision is what has been driving

Team Rapha in Majorca. Photograph by Emily Maye, courtesy of Rapha

me, that's why there haven't been leaps. It has also been important to have been the first to see the market. I think we caught the wave before people knew it was happening – 7 or 8 years ago people starting talking about road cycling, The Times and The FT first started writing about it and talking about cycling being 'the new golf' and that

felt like the massive breakthrough."
Rapha's style divides the road cycling community somewhat, as Simon explains. *"We do annoy people, some people get quite upset about our attitude and we're quite 'out there'. Rapha is not positioned as your best mate, we're not warm and cuddly. We think like the customer when we are* developing products but we don't position ourselves as the customer. We like to lead the customer, show, reveal and introduce people to things and take them on a wonderful journey. That adds a degree of tension, we always like to be one step ahead. We have a leader's attitude and we are pretty uncompromising. There is also

Courtesy of Rapha

a certain darkness about Rapha, that goes right back to what cycling is all about. The real appeal of road cycling for those who participate in it is actually the suffering, not the pleasure. Yes, the bikes are great and you get the thrill, but it doesn't mean anything unless you've suffered to get there, physically and mentally. Cycling can be so tough it's awful; I was standing on the side of the road, watching a race in Italy the other week, and the racers looked at me much as soldiers would if you watched them marching to war. They were covered in grime, they were at their limit; it was painful and not beautiful. I thought I shouldn't be here witnessing this; that I was intruding on their own private pain. We often use black and white photography and talk about the psychological aspects of the sport and hint at this relationship between suffering and glory. Because cycling is so hard, our attitude has always been that there should be no reason to compromise between the form and performance and style of the products and the experience. We make no apology for wanting cyclists to

look great, the sport's tough but it's amazing and I want to look great when I am doing it. When we do things well, we do them with humility, creativity and with quality. Some people recognise that what we are doing is valuable, and do like it. We are very polarising and I am happy that we are."

There is an intensity in the attention to detail when Rapha presents itself — whether through its products, or its stories and films representing the sport.

"We're often seen as quite a romantic brand, we don't lead with the technology, we lead with the emotion of an amazing photograph, the moment, the experience, and we're very happy to be quite romantic about it, because it is a romantic sport and the experience that you sometimes have on your best days on a racing bike is romantic too. Often, we're criticised for being overly romantic and not being backed up by real performance and real technology. But the people who think that are not Rapha customers; our customers

Photograph by Wig Worland, courtesy of Rapha

get it. The performance and technology are there in spades, but they are not the primary connection we make with customers and the sport. It is an interesting balance; emotional films and photography with a rational underpinning."

As one of the sport's magazines, *Cycle & Style*, reports: '... the clothing is favoured for its high performance, comfort and attention to detail. It may be a joke that some people have engraved on their identity wrist band, "Don't cut my shorts — they're Rapha!"[84]

As well as the technology inherent in Rapha products, there are also hidden details such as the labelling of Rapha's clothing — each product contains a story on the label, a narrative inspired by the legends and characters of the sport. For the launch of Rapha, Simon even got his mother to make him a shirt out of some of these labels — slightly uncomfortable to wear but very on-brand and stylish. It seems that this attention to detail,

telling the story of the sport — communicating the glory and suffering — has paid off. From January 2013, Rapha is the official clothing provider to the Sky Pro Cycling team. They will provide a complete range of clothing and accessories to dress Team Sky — the world's highest ranked team — both on and off the bike. Dave Brailsford, Team Principal of Sky Pro Cycling, had this to say: "Team Sky has achieved this year's level of success because of a strong and steady vision to find improvement at every level to help our riders win. I see Rapha joining us next year as another step in that direction. They share our ambition and vision for cycling."[85]

Now that's a good story, and a happy ending.

Applying the human hand

Donald Duck was created in 1934 and famously quacked the catchphrase "What's the big idea?". It seems we have been asking ourselves the same question ever since. Business growth is nourished on a diet of big ideas: fast food, self-service, the World Wide Web, budget air travel, the tablet computer. But big ideas don't singlehandedly make a business successful. People don't go to supermarkets and fill their shopping carts with big ideas. Vision alone is not enough. Big ideas have to be translated into products, services and experiences that are capable of creating happiness. More often than not, this means that big ideas need to be accompanied by a set of smaller ideas that add meat to the bone. The delight is in the detail.

Courtesy of DDB

Volkswagen has long understood that small details can make a big difference. Long before Apple urged the world to "think different", VW introduced America to the concept of "think small". One of the company's most iconic pieces of communication champions the attention to detail of the quality control inspectors working at its Wolfsburg factor in Germany. It tells the story of Kurt Kroner, who out of 3,389 inspectors identified a blemished chrome strip on the glove compartment of a Beetle. On the strength of a flaw that most customers would never notice, the car was publicly branded a "lemon". Since then, Volkswagen has demonstrated a passion for detail bordering on the obsessive, even going as far as perfecting the sound its doors make as they are slammed shut. Unreasonable amounts of time and money are invested in honing aspects of the driving experience that most drivers barely notice.

Volkswagen isn't alone in obsessing about detail. Leica Camera is another business with a sharp sense of focus. In a world where cameras are frequently sold on the basis of countless frills and features, Leica concentrates on the details that are most essential to creating a flawless experience. A standard Leica lens is made up of 100 individual parts, assembled and finished by hand and rigorously tested once complete. The cumulative result of each carefully crafted detail is what can only be described as reverence on the part of celebrated photographers, including Henri Cartier-Bresson, Robert Doisneau and Elliott Erwitt. Discerning customers clearly care about such details.

Professional customers aside, for the majority of people it seems absurd to attach such disproportionate importance to details such as the noise a car door makes as it slams or whether a camera lens surround is hand-lacquered. It seems even stranger when we consider the amount of time and energy invested in perfecting these details. Nobody buys a car based on the sound of a slamming door, or a camera because the manufacturer's logo has been hand-mounted. And no amount of market research or customer journey analysis will justify making these investments. Such commitment to craft defies rationalisation through cost-benefit or ROI analysis. But this lack of rationality is precisely why getting these details right is so important: they demonstrate thoughtfulness on the part of a business. Knowing that VW cares about the chrome finish on a glove compartment reassures us that the rest of the car must be the result of an exacting engineering process. Leica cameras are expected to outlive their owners – a rare occurrence in today's throwaway society.

Getting the details right is not a luxury. It's the difference between being tolerated and being desired

Getting the details right is not a luxury. It's the difference between being tolerated and being desired. Great products and services may be born out of big ideas, but what people experience is a series of details. It makes sense to pay the most attention to the most important of these elements, but ignoring the myriad tiny facets that also make up this experience increases the chances that you'll annoy people over time. This is being typed on a MacBook Pro, which the people at Apple designed with some pretty sharp lines. The product looks fantastic. But after the first few thousand words, those same sharp lines reveal themselves to be perfectly positioned for scraping against your wrists. Similar niggles are a common feature of daily life, but just as small details can make a big difference, minor errors can have far-reaching implications.

This point is vividly illustrated by the very public mistakes made by some car manufacturers in naming their vehicles. These include a Mitsubishi SUV launched in 1982, which was named "Pajero" after *Leopardus pajeros*, the Pampas cat which is native to the Patagonia plateau region of southern Argentina.[86] Unfortu-nately, since "Pajero" is an offensive term in Spanish, Mitsubishi has employed alternative names in international markets, adding unnecessary cost and complexity to an already diverse product range. Toyota made a similar mistake with their MR2 sportscar, which was simply named "MR" in France, because of the similarity in pronunciation of "MR2" with the French slang word "merdeux".

Brand naming seems to be the Achilles' heel of many a great business. Apple Computer has repeatedly clashed with other businesses over the trademark rights to the names of its company and products. As early as 1978, Apple Computer was the subject of a trademark infringement lawsuit filed by The Beatles' Apple Corps. The suit was settled in 1981 for US$80,000, plus an agreement that Apple Computer would not enter into the music business.[87] Decades of legal wrangles over the right to use the Apple name ensued, culminating in Apple Computer's buyout of Apple Corps' trademark rights in 2007 for an estimated US$500 million.[88] In the same year, Apple's launch of the iPhone prompted a legal wrangle with Cisco, which had previously owned the right to use the iPhone trademark. Few of these details are critical to the success or failure of the businesses involved. A substandard glove compartment cover does not fundamentally compromise the performance of a VW Beetle. Nor is the appeal of the iPhone dramatically influenced by its name: it's difficult to argue that the iCall, ApplePhone or the iMobile would have been any less successful. Getting details right is hard and can be both costly and time-consuming. But getting these details wrong can be even more expensive, as well as denting confidence in the businesses involved.

...the faults and foibles we come to cherish in the people around us become evidence of sloppiness and ineptitude when we encounter them in a business...

When it comes to people, we may find imperfection to be a source of charm, character and individuality. But the faults and foibles we come to cherish in the people around us become evidence of sloppiness and ineptitude when we encounter them in a business; for example, dealing with call centres about something deeply personal, where even your recorded details are inaccurate. When businesses overlook the importance of such details, they reveal some of the worst aspects of humanity: laziness, carelessness, sometimes even contempt. But when they make the effort to get these small details right, they provide us with a valuable spark of humanity that draws us to them. Whole Foods is a master of this art, punctuating their shopping experience with a series of delightful little touches that radiate warmth, personality and humanity: chalkboards featuring handwritten messages about the store's employees and producers; storage containers that add texture and interest to the produce; cashiers who examine eggs to ensure that none are cracked. Individually, these details don't amount to much. But cumulatively, they have generated an almost cult-like appeal, not to mention paying back commercially. For a typical supermarket, it's reasonable to expect sales of around US$400 per square foot. Whole Foods achieves more than double this figure.[89] It pays to be personal.

In Japan, the concept of "wabi-sabi" embraces the beauty of irregularity. It celebrates idiosyncratic production techniques, which result in unique experiences. Wabi-sabi invites us to consider the tiny details that set an object apart from all other objects: beauty is not a matter of ordered perfection, but of individuality and impermanence.

It is little wonder that "Loopwheel" machines are a thing of the past. They are capable of producing only 12 metres of fabric per day; the equivalent output of a modern rapier loom is closer to 10,000 metres per day.[90] They are also bulky, noisy and require constant attention from skilled craftsmen. But there's a benefit to being slow: the speed of modern machines creates excess tension, which impacts the texture of the cloth. Loopwheel machines use only the tension provided by gravity, with the result that "it feels as if air has been knitted into the material."[91] Around 200 loopwheel machines remain and the overwhelming majority of these supply a single business in Japan: Loopwheeler.

Loopwheeler make sweatshirts with a devotion to traditional methods that borders on the obsessive. The fabric is sewn together using a "flat seam" sewing machine, which uses six threads at a time to improve the durability of the product. This is not tradition for its own sake; each step in the process has a clear benefit over modern mass production techniques. And the result is conspicuously modern; crewneck and hooded sweaters, as well as collaborations with brands like Nike and Harris Tweed.

But Loopwheeler's success is not a triumph of process. Founder and owner, Satoshi Suzuki, acknowledges that the company's achievements are down to the skills of the people he works with:

> What is the most important for Loopwheeler is the mindset of our staff. They are actually seeing every stitch of every Loopwheeler product as it is made and are obsessed with fine-tuning the formula for the thickness of the thread, gauge and mesh count. Each piece of Loopwheeler product is made by hand and finished with their affection.

It's very difficult to fake this level of attention and commitment. Each item has a story; it is the culmination of years of attention and refinement. The human touch shows through. It needs to: Loopwheeler sweaters can cost over US$200. Fans of the brand pay for the quality and durability of the garment, but they also understand that they are supporting a noble approach to making garments that went out of fashion a long time ago.

The more human a business feels to its employees and customers, the more likely it is to elicit a positive response. Some businesses go to great lengths to provide moments of delight, no matter how small, no matter how momentary. Chanel No. 5 bottles are sealed using a process called "baudruchage" in which a fine membrane and cord are wrapped around the bottle's neck and sealed with a wax cachet. The back of every pack of Burts hand-fried potato chips bears the name of the fryer who made them. These businesses create a sense of intimacy and wonder that can't be faked by a marketing department. Every point of contact a business has with its audiences is an opportunity to surprise and delight, an opportunity to elevate our experience of that business above the humdrum.

Oticon
The art of listening

In 1902, Hans Demant was shown a picture of the Danish-born Crown Princess Alexandra on the day of her coronation in London. Barely noticeable amongst the rich folds of mink and silk, the elaborate webs of pearls and jewels, the new Queen of England wore one of the world's first hearing aids.

The following year Mr Demant set sail for England to buy the same type of hearing device, driven by a desire to help his wife Camilla, who had experienced hearing loss at a young age. Since the Demant family began importing and distributing electronic hearing devices in 1904, Oticon's stature as one of the world's leading manufacturers and providers of hearing devices has grown rapidly and resolutely.

Today Oticon is amongst the three largest providers of hearing care solutions in the world, with operations in more than 30 countries and sales activities all over the world. Its track record of innovative product launches has established a formidable technical reputation. Oticon is proud of its 'firsts'. In 1992 it introduced the world's first fully automatic hearing device. Since then, Oticon has created the world's first fully digital device and the world's first device with high-performance wireless technologies. Seen from the outside, Oticon appears to be a company that places technology first. But within a few minutes of meeting Søren Nielsen, the company's President, it becomes apparent that technology is, as he puts it, just the tip of the iceberg.

"In our industry, technology plays a large role and those that master that technology are generally seen as leaders in the industry. Our promise includes a product

Princess Alexandra on the day of her coronation in London, 1902

but it is not limited to that product. Our mission and role is to support the personal interaction between the hearing-care professional and the end user, to play a supporting role in better understanding the individual challenges and tailoring a personalised solution."

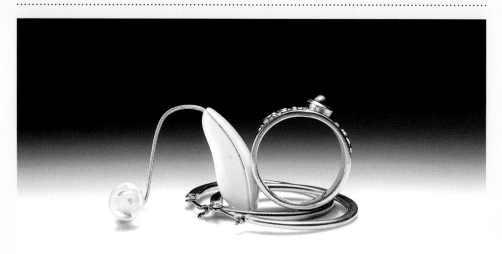

Courtesy of Oticon

Oticon's technological prowess is just the icing on the cake. What sets Oticon apart is empathy. In everything Oticon does, each action and interaction, a human hand guides. It is a business based on relationships and a deep understanding of the people it works with and works for.

"Since the company was started, we have been dedicated and completely focused on truly understanding what life is like with a hearing impairment and what it is like to be a hearing care specialist, interacting with people that are hard of hearing.

Two people with theoretically exactly the same hearing loss react very differently to different settings. Some people can handle a very dynamic hearing aid that can pick up sounds from all different kinds of angles and others prefer a more calm and steady system. Being able to counsel that, to understand the nuances and to find out what precise solution works for the individual is of huge importance."

Not content to rely on reports mediated through hearing care professionals and consultants, the company deploys its own support and research teams to observe how people interact with their products and consultants, deep-diving into personal experiences, emotional challenges and practical details. Members of Oticon's sales and support staff spend over an hour with hearing care professionals, at least once every two to three months. Oticon have established a state-of-the-art independent research centre committed to deepening their understanding of the real-life implications of hearing loss and sharing those findings with others.

"We strongly believe that investing resources in deep-diving into these experiences and challenges feeds our ability to create solutions that are in tune with the needs of both the end-users and the hearing care professionals. The fact is that half of the people who go to a hearing care professional and are diagnosed with hearing loss still choose not to buy anything. We need to understand the barriers. How can we change the profile of hearing impairment or the way we present our solutions?'

Understanding the individual experiences of hearing loss is only one world that Oticon immerses itself in. The company has a clear sense of its role in supporting the relationship between hearing care professionals and their patients.

"I think that what we do really well is supporting specialists in understanding these practical, psychological and emotional experiences of the individual. We see a significant change in the mind-set of the consumer of the products that we create. People are looking for a counsellor, not a medical advisor. They don't like to be told what is right, they want to be involved in decision-making. This is very different to 10 or 15 years ago when it was a very prescriptive model. This change in behaviour creates a need and demand from the hearing care professional in getting better support, better tools, so they can do a better job. We really see ourselves as partners with our customers. We want our customers to be the most professional and the best in the industry. Through providing marketing tools, open-house seminars, knowledge exchange programmes, we support them in becoming that."

This 'listening ear' and earnest, compassionate approach guides every relationship the company has, from end-users and hearing care professionals to the company's rapport with its own employees.

"Our people first mission — that same mission to better understand the elements of people's experience of having and treating hearing loss - it is something that our employees are part of. We try to get everyone to share in this mission. We want everyone to have a relatively high level of understanding of the business that we are in. People are kept motivated and like to do what they do. We are good at creating a picture of where we can do better and where we can win the battle."

For many companies with such a strong culture and sense of internal motivation, partnership, mergers and acquisitions are often a minefield of tensions, frustrations and often, departures. Over the past 8 years, the owner of Oticon, William Demant Holding, have welcomed around 70 successful companies into their group. Nielsen does not claim these successes for the 'Oticon culture'. Despite immense pride in the culture of his organisation, Nielsen expresses characteristic humility in his reflection of this history of successful ventures. Even in these potentially highly contentious affairs, it seems that empathy and respect have been the guiding principles for Oticon and the bed-rock for its stellar record.

"If you buy something, you have seen a value in it that you don't already have. You don't want to change it with injections of your own culture. Typically, you share a certain perspective already. There are of course fundamental standards that we expect: transparent management, open-minded thinking, a sustainable, long-term approach. But beyond this, we don't go in with a SWAT team of Oticon people. Then we would lose the people for which the company was bought. We don't buy companies for assets, we buy them for people. If the people leave, the assets leave."

Ultimately Oticon's success is the sum of its parts; strong leadership, a deep sense of internal motivation and shared purpose amongst employees, market-leading technological innovation and a professional, integrated service. But underlying each of these elements and binding them together is Oticon's profound empathy, its willingness to listen to the people that the organisation works with and works for.

An important factor in the profundity of the Oticon culture can be found in the

Courtesy of Oticon

unique ownership structure where Oticon's main shareholder, the Oticon Foundation, has approximately 60% of the shares of William Demant Holding. This constellation eases some of the pressure for short-term results which a company listed on the stock exchange may face and enables a long-term focus. Even though the demand to perform is still strong, the affiliation to the Oticon Foundation nurtures the awareness of the deep roots — in this case the shared story of the Demant family.

Furthermore, the Oticon Foundation each year contributes around EUR 10 million to charitable causes, and many of these donations are connected to the provenance of the Oticon business — audiology. This important facet also supports the unique sense of pride in the

culture, the awareness that the company, in fact, makes the world a better place.

"Uniqueness — it is about culture. It is deeply engrained in everything you do. When I think of Oticon and what sets it apart, I think of the analogy of the iceberg. You can see a few facts on the surface but it is really what is underwater that makes the difference."

Developing a signature style

David Ogilvy was a big fan of signatures. He believed that we try harder when the work we produce bears our name:

> I believe that all copy should be signed by the agency. This is never done in the United States, on the ground that manu-facturers buy space to advertise their products, not their agencies. Short-sighted. My experience suggests that when agencies sign their ads, they produce better ones. When Reader's Digest asked me to write an advertisement for their magazine, they specified that I had to sign it. Golly did I work hard on that ad. Everyone was going to know who wrote it.[92]

There's a lovely idea here: when we add our signature to some-thing, we demonstrate our belief in its worth. Painters are expected to sign their work for the same reason. When we put our name to something we've created, then we do our best to make sure it represents our own definition of what great looks like. It becomes a statement about who we are and what we believe. We become identified with the work that bears our name and we are judged as a result. If this sounds dramatic, consider that during his editorship of *Interview* magazine, Andy Warhol signed a set of copies of the magazine that would ordinarily retail for US$2. He charged buyers US$50 for the signed magazines, which quickly sold out. Warhol's aim was to demonstrate that our obsession with celebrity had reached a point of absurdity, because he assumed that his signature had no intrinsic value. But why shouldn't his signature add value to the work? By his own admission, the act of signing the magazines elevated them from mere glossies into works of conceptual art. When we apply our signature to a piece of work, we confer a sense of value on that work that didn't exist before. The people who bought the signed copies of the magazine weren't buying a magazine at all. They were buying something far more valuable: a work of art endorsed personally by Andy Warhol.

This is about creating more than superficial "badge value". Many Leica owners tape over the distinctive red dot on their cameras to reduce the likelihood of theft. Few – if any – remove the dot entirely. The prominence of the company's mark on its products communicates a confidence in their quality and establishes a sense of pride in their creation. When a company provides such a visible demonstration of the value it places on its own work, then the people who view or buy that work are more likely to value it themselves.

But signatures aren't just evidence of pride, or communicators of value. They are also carriers of meaning. They lend a sense of character and personality to the item that bears them. Anthro-pologist Marcel Danesi considers signatures to be "the epitome of individuality".[93] This goes far beyond placing a red dot on a camera, or signing-off a piece of copy in an advertisement. Beautiful businesses imbue every aspect of their work with meaning: they create a signature style.

When a company provides such a visible demonstration of the value it places on its own work, then the people who view or buy that work are more likely to value it themselves.

Cultivating a signature style doesn't make a business silly or superficial. Gore Vidal pointed out that "Style is a matter of knowing who you are, what you want to say, and not giving a damn."[94] *The Economist* magazine operates in an extremely sober field of business, where credibility is a precondition for success. Readers must be able to trust the veracity of its news and have faith in the integrity of its views. It's easy to think of a signature style as a distraction from the serious business of news delivery, but *The Economist* faces significant competition for the attention of its readers from publications such as *BusinessWeek*, *The Wall Street Journal* and the *Financial Times*, not to mention the myriad sources of news online. The news is the same, so the style in which this news is delivered is critical to standing out in a crowded area. And *The Economist* certainly isn't afraid of standing out. The contents page of each edition carries the following message:

First published in September 1843, to take part in "a severe contest between intelligence, which presses forward, and an unworthy, timid ignorance obstructing our progress."

According to *The Economist* website, the newspaper considers itself to be "the enemy of privilege, pomposity and predictability". This forthright sentiment is mirrored in its bold red masthead, as well as its unapologetic use of provocative wit, most immediately evident on its front cover, in its headlines and illustrations, not to mention the lines the newspaper has used over the years to attract readers:

Is your indecision final?

Trump Donald.

Some like it yacht.

A poster should contain no more than eight words, which is the maximum the average reader can take at a single glance. This, however, is for Economist readers.

Because fences make uncomfortable seats.

Leaders' digest.

To err is human. To er, um, ah is unacceptable.

Avoid the pedestrian.

Not all mind expanding substances are illegal.

The Economist doesn't like to share its signature. Its editor and authors write anonymously: it is a byline-free environment. "Many hands write *The Economist*, but it speaks with a collective voice."[95] This voice is revealed in its eponymous style guide, which has become a bible for people who want to communicate clearly in English. Although *The Economist* has attracted an army of one and a half million readers – as well as featuring in an episode of The Simpsons – not everybody is a fan. James Fallows, writing in the *Washington Post* in 1991, seemed particularly annoyed by *The Economist*'s distinctive tone of voice:

> In America, the magazine presents itself as a kind of voice of the super-confident English aristocracy, whereas its advertisements within England play on the status-anxiety of its readers there. For example, one billboard displayed in England reads in bold print: "I never read *The Economist*." The punch line comes in the identification of the hapless confessor of this dereliction, a "Management trainee – aged 44."

> The other ugly English trait promoting *The Economist's* success in America is the Oxford Union argumentative style. At its epitome, it involves a stance so cocksure of its rightness and superiority that it would be a shame to freight it with mere fact.

It just goes to show: you can't please all of the people all of the time. Nor does *The Economist* try to: its signature style is designed to appeal to a very specific group of readers. Gore Vidal would have been proud.

Condé Nast
A talent for quality

For over 100 years, Condé Nast has been at the heart of magazine publishing, with titles such as *Vogue*, *The New Yorker* and *Vanity Fair* demonstrating their commitment to the highest quality and relevance of content in each and every one of their publications.

We spoke to Xavier Romatet, CEO of Condé Nast France to explore these values: *"Three things characterize our business. First, we are a brand business. At Condé Nast, we believe in the capability for success, not only of the magazines but of the brands. This is very important. For us, the magazines are a way to support something that brings extra value, which is the brand. That's what makes up the singularity and special nature of this business. Worldwide, Condé Nast is the press group with the highest number of international brands. Vogue is in 20 countries, GQ is in 15 countries and Glamour is in 18 countries, Vanity Fair (6 countries), AD (8 countries) and Condé Nast Traveler (8 countries). We believe in the value of brands. It is a reference for our readers and advertisers. These values are all the stronger because they are shared across the world.*

"Our business model is based on this premise. Firstly, the value of our brands starts with product quality, like a luxury brand. Could Chanel continue to sell if the Chanel brand was no longer synonymous with something extra — social status, dreams, excellence, quality — and if product production quality were compromised in times of crisis, where corners would be cut on leather quality or manufacturing time? Product quality is something we never hesitate about. Vogue is the emblematic brand and probably the most expensive

magazine to produce. This costs a lot. If, instead of working with a less recognized photographer who costs less, I'm going to maximize short-term profit, but I'm going to lessen Vogue's overall value as a brand which depends on quality. So, our business model is based on long-lasting quality.

"Secondly, we make specific choices — for example strong editorial choices. Vogue presents photos or contents which are not subject to mutual consensus. I often say that the Vogue brand must be a devilish brand. This is because the artistic license and creative freedom we give to our stylists and photographers are an essential condition to attract them and to stand out from the crowd. It's this difference that creates preference. In a world where everything is tending toward uniformity, we get a different and an original point of view from specific choices, and these are what I use to create the image, the reputation, the difference and eventually the preference.

"The third element is 'unexpectedness'. For each issue, Vogue must be where it's not expected to be. People must ask themselves: 'What are they going to surprise me with this month?' The artistic search must be unending. The theme, the cover selection, the choices must be different. One month, we can be extremely classic, stylish and elegant, and the next month on the cutting edge, extremist and controversial. In the end, the best compliment we can hear is: 'Only Vogue can do that!'"

Courtesy of Condé Nast

Condé Nast is, of course, an international business, with great consistency and recognition through their different titles across the world; we asked how they achieved this.

"One of the strengths of the Group is that a myriad of companies are motivated by two characteristics, which would seem to be contradictory:

> ➤ *Respect for brand values, which is universal;*
> ➤ *Total freedom to adapt them to their local environment.*

"We have very strong structuring values and total creative and entreprenurial freedom in Condé Nast Group. There's a sort of constant tension behind our success, which obliges us to respect brand values at the worldwide level, and being fully able to use the best means in each of our countries. For this reason, Vogue Italy is not the same as Vogue Paris, which is not the same as Vogue U.S.

Each month, there are as many Vogues as there are countries. We have tools to assist us in creating international databases. We have Vogue exporters and Vogue importers. Vogue in Paris is one of the most used by other countries, who can then reproduce its content. Paris remains a reference for the world.

Developing a signature style | Condé Nast

This facilitates our global expansion whilst helping smaller countries that don't have the resource or the history to launch. For example, probably when we launch Vogue Thailand next year, we will see photos from the most famous photographers, giving Vogue Thailand a status and position in its market that is superior to other magazines. And our covers are unique. I don't remember having re-used a cover from one country to another. The brand's strength comes from the fact that it has a universal status and reputation and a totally local execution."

The way the group is structured has helped Condé Nast in its international expansion: "Something surprised me very much, in the positive sense, when I became part of this Group. First of all, there is no international structure: there is no international financial or strategy director and no international headquarters. Each country has a boss, who is an entrepreneur. The decision-making process is of an entrepreneurial nature; the one who decides is the shareholder. When shareholders go to a country, when they visit France, we spend most of our time looking at the products and speak less of P&L and financial constraints, because shareholders feel that income is a consequence of the product. The Group asset is the value of its brands, and the value of its brands is the quality of its products. Brand value is greatly superior to operating P&L for the year. Operating P&L for the year is a consequence of brand value."

Condé Nast has great coherency in quality and presence on shelf, and Xavier Romatet explains: "This is because the people who are in charge of coherency are all aware of their great responsibility. For the most part, this brand has been around for a long time and has an incredible history. In France, it's been here for 92 years, in the United States, 97 years. We are only the inheritors of something that was built before we arrived on the scene. And our job is to serve something that already exists.

Managers of the Group are not financiers first but Brand builders or Brand developers.

"Vogue is one of the world's oldest magazines. History has left us a heritage; we need to ensure it bears fruit. Therefore, we are perfectly aware of the responsibility we have to keep serving a history which was born before us and will continue after us. People are absolutely key, and the magazine writers and editors who are Brand Managers are keenly, absolutely and totally aware of the value of the brands they are working for. The Group pays careful attention to the fact that the magazine editors-in-chief and publishers are people who fundamentally share brand values. I think that coherence comes much more from a culture than a system. Culture is people rather than the system.

"Talent is often associated with a charismatic and demanding personality. We see it as an opportunity for the group. We are absolutely not afraid to have extremely strong personalities. Our magazines' history is full of them. As long as the personalities serve the brand, we accept the need to manage creative talents, with everything that entails in terms of ego and the spotlight. If we think something is going off-course and that the personality overwhelms the brand, then we don't compromise. This is the reason why we separated from Carine Roitfeld eighteen months ago: not because she didn't have talent — she has incredible talent — but because her personal vision for the brand began to take the place of Vogue's universal vision. And when 'personal' takes the place of "universal", everything we talked about before begins to go off-course. These personalities must understand that they are at the service of the brands and not the other way round.

"70% of Vogue revenue comes from advertising, and 60% of advertising revenue comes from fashion. The rest comes from beauty, jewellery, watchmaking, and so on.

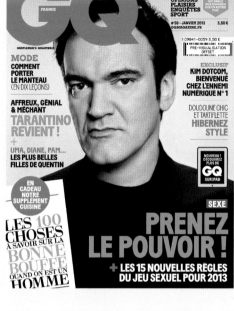

Courtesy of Condé Nast

We are in a two-tier system. Some of the people we talk about are also the people who finance us. In fashion, it's exacerbated because there is visibility, money, egos and some very complicated relationships. We are very much aware of this. It's not LVMH who decides the content policy for Vogue Paris or Vogue U.S. Yes, LVMH is the Group's leading client. Each side has its work to do. The people who write the editorials must be perfectly aware of the fact that LVMH is the world's leading luxury Group. This awareness doesn't restrict our freedom but increases our responsibility."

Xavier explained the business model that forms the basis for Condé Nast: *"Our model is based on the fact that we chose a niche which has one notable characteristic: narrowness. This niche is always in high-end lifestyle. When we select a niche, we always enter it with conviction and a need to create the best product, always keeping in mind that the goal is to be the leader of reference. The leader of reference is not the one with*

the largest circulation number; it's the one who has the greatest influence. If Vogue, Vanity Fair, GQ, Condé Nast Traveler and The New Yorker have such an outstanding reputation, it's because of their influence. Today, we are influential because we are perceived as being the best made. We are more than just observers on each sector; we are often people involved by our actions, our events, our ranking, and our influence. We influence a lot of brand designers and stylists because they often tell us: 'In Vogue, I find things that will influence what I do in my next collection.

"We never show fashion like many women's magazines do, by illustrating their pages with runway photos. We re-create something from our intuition, the talent of our fashion editors and the worldwide photographers we work with. We are both a creative player, for the design aspect, and a business player because we influence our readers and the market. Our magazines play the role of trendsetters. By placing brands in Vogue, we have a media

function for reaching a certain audience, but we also have an image function: we offer brands an image and a status they wouldn't have if they were in another magazine. It's precisely this brand model that enables us to build our business model on values. We cost a lot, and our products cost a lot per issue for the consumer and the advertiser, because we provide added value, which is the added value of the brand. This is why our shareholders are so concerned about product quality. If we lowered product quality, our business model would collapse."

This obsession with quality and distinction is what gives Condé Nast its lasting, characteristic signature in the crowded world of publishing.

Courtesy of Condé Nast

Creating a sense of theatre

The themes explored so far in this chapter – storytelling, attention to detail and the development of a signature style – culminate in an experience. This experience can be intellectual or aesthetic, or both. Arguably, the ideal experience is a combination of the two: an appeal to both the heart and the mind. Great experiences sing to every sense. Regardless of whether we are employees, customers or marginally interested bystanders, our impression of a business is the result of an accumulation of discrete interactions with it. Our impression of Starbucks is formed from more than just the taste of its coffee: it's a combination of the charisma of Howard Schultz, the ubiquity and uniformity of its coffee shops, the amount of time we spend queuing, the attitude of its staff, the comfort of its seats, the speed of its service, the absurd size of its cups and countless other points of interaction that we stand little chance of listing on fewer than ten pages.

The context in which we experience a product or service has a profound effect on how much we enjoy it and how vividly and fondly we remember it. A little imagination can go a long way. Theatre shows people that you care about what you're doing. It also exhibits sensitivity to your business' audiences. Why not try to make every interaction delightful? Businesses create wonderful experiences when they sing to every sense.

Unfortunately, enjoyment and memorability don't seem to be too high on the agenda of many businesses. Our sense of theatre rarely extends beyond an interesting slide transition on a PowerPoint presentation, or the inclusion of an imposing atrium at the entrance of our buildings. Business is a serious affair and credibility is king. Fluff and fanfare are to be avoided at all costs. We would prefer to be dull than to risk seeming foolish. Which is a shame. We put so much time and effort into creating the perfect strategy, idea, product, service or proposition, that we frequently neglect the way in which we choose to present our work. But some people dare to be different.

Salvador Dali had a keen sense of theatre. In the 1940s he was commissioned by Max Factor to create a brand name and a bottle for their latest perfume. Dali accepted the commission but refused to follow any of the procedures most designers would consider useful in achieving a successful result. He refused to meet his client. He showed no interest in developing an understanding of the product itself, its target audience, where it was to be sold or how it was to be marketed. His only stipulation (presumably apart from a gargantuan fee) was that he should be given four weeks, after which a press conference should be held in New York's finest hotel. Then and then only would Dali reveal his design. Four weeks later, the world's press descended upon the Astoria Hotel on Fifth Avenue, flashbulbs at the ready.

Dali arrived nearly an hour late, visibly bereft of any object resembling a perfume bottle. As he strode towards the lectern, journalists fired questions while flashbulbs were discharged all around him. Just before he reached the lectern, Dali conjured a handkerchief from his pocket and bent over to pick up a still-glowing expended flashbulb. He pressed the bulb gently against the lectern to flatten its tip and paused to allow it to cool. Once the bulb was cold enough to handle, Dali held it aloft and announced, "Ladies and Gentlemen, I give you Max Factor's 'Electrique'!" Dali's homage to Christopher Columbus shows how a little theatre can go a long way.

Great experiences sing to every sense.

When Josef Sachs founded the Swedish department store NK in 1902, his ambition was to create a "cultural and commercial theatre". The business thinks of its department stores in Stockholm and Göteborg as stages and it seeks to put the products they sell in the spotlight. The aim of the business is to give its visitors something for free: a sense of wonder and occasion that adds value to the products it sells. As far as NK is concerned, theatre isn't just the icing on top of the cake. NK is very restrictive in its use of price reductions and discounts to attract business: these approaches demonstrate a lack of confidence in the quality of its products.

This means that many of the products it sells are available more cheaply elsewhere and on the internet. But it's difficult to create a sense of drama over the internet. Theatre isn't simply the ambition of the business: theatre is its principal source of competitive advantage against discounters and online retailers. And the results can be stunning. Bloggers claim that its "hyperfabulous" Stockholm food hall "will blow most foodies away"[96] and Concierge.com describes the store as "unquestionably the best, most elegant department store in town".[97] Even NK's in-store pharmacy employs theatre to attract crowds: its 2012 advertising campaign employed high fashion models and photography to produce a stylish take on common ailments. Back pain and blisters have never seemed sexier.

NK isn't alone in understanding the power of a theatrical retail experience. Selfridges in London has a 19,000 square foot "Wonder Room" dedicated to showcasing hyper-luxury items designed to take your breath away. Burberry has recently re-launched its flagship store in London to create a new way for people to interact with the business, its products and craftsmanship. Luxury businesses frequently employ theatre to create a sense of drama and to stimulate interest, but they aren't the only businesses that appreciate the importance of cultivating an immersive experience.

Bloomberg L.P. is about as serious as business gets. According to its website, more than 20 million of us visit Bloomberg news sites each month and the company answers just under 12,000 analytics questions an hour. In 2009, Bloomberg was estimated to control a third of the global financial data market,[98] which was estimated at the time to be worth US$16 billion. Despite the importance of the digital world to the dissemination all of this data, at the heart of Bloomberg's success is a belief in the importance of its physical environments on the quality of the work it produces. The idea is simple: to create unique and vibrant working spaces that promote the creation of unique and vibrant content. Each of the business' offices embodies its cultural values: transparency and openness, connectivity, colour and drama. Spaces are designed to encourage interaction and information sharing. In a 1995 interview with Fast Company, Michael Bloomberg explained the importance of physical space:

> What I'm selling is information... The best way to get it faster than anyone else is to create an environment of constant creativity. You have to turn up the volume, make people a little uncomfortable.[99]

In the same way that NK thinks of its stores as a stage, Bloomberg's offices are a platform from which information is created. Every feature is designed with this end in mind. Staircases aren't just for walking between floors — they are vertical meeting spaces. Working spaces are purposefully small — not to save space but to encourage people to share ideas. Theatre is a vital business tool in the battle against the humdrum. It's an opportunity to provide valuable context for the work a business carries out. To demonstrate purpose and to create a sense of unity. Style and substance aren't contradictory forces, but complementary assets for enlightened businesses.

Story
Retail media

Take a gallery, retail store, community centre, magazine and billboard and combine them with storytelling, events and shopping and you will arrive at 144 10th Avenue at 19th Street in New York. A buzzing, friendly, contemporary retail store, Story.

Courtesy of Story

Founder, Rachel Shechtman has conjured up this innovative business model for a new kind of retailing. The Story store is reinvented every 4-8 weeks around a chosen theme and celebrates versatility and community engagement.

"I would hope that if someone's favourite magazine could come to life, it would be our store. Our version of editorial is the merchandise that we curate around a theme and the events that we host; and we also have the publishing, which is the sponsorship. So an example of that is our

Story Colour; our editorial mix had a thousand units merchandised by colour, we did events like 'Learn How to Change your Mood with the Colour you Paint your Home in' and then the sponsor on the publishing side was paint producer, Benjamin Moore.

"The objective of the stories is to have wide and broad appeal. I have two rules, one is that any story has to be relevant to someone who 5 years old or 80 years old and the other that we are an environment that is able to sell something for $5 or

$5,000. As long as I meet those two rules, we look at the time of year, our potential partners and start to develop a story. For example last spring we thought; it's summer time, there are lots of tourists — what will appeal to locals and tourists? Let's do Story New York, we'll have things designed and made by New Yorkers, everything will be New York themed."

Between each Story, the store closes for between 5-14 days to transform itself, the windows are covered up and used for campaign messaging and then re-opened and revealed to the public.

"We also don't release the next story to our customers — just like you don't know what is on the cover of the magazine before it comes out. This ultimately becomes a 'surprise and delight' factor, and it's a good way to get people to join your data base, because they come in and ask about the next story and though we don't tell them — we can put them on our invitation list."

After consulting for over 10 years, Rachel felt that apart from a selection of companies such as Apple and Anthropologie, the retail space had largely been ignored as a space for innovation.

"At Story I hope we are as much a community centre as a store in our customers' eyes. One moment you could be doing exercise classes in here, in another you could be making robots on MakerBot 3D printers and another making fresh pasta with an Italian grandmother from Staten Island during our New York Story."

At Story, Rachel creates a sense of theatre with the pace of change, the reveal process and by emphasising on building a rapport with visitors. She has also identified a shift in how Story stores have triggered how retailing is done:

"Historically, people competed on price, quality and service; now, that is a 'need to have' not a 'nice to have'. My 70/30 rule is that 30% is surprise and delight, which is critical and can come in many forms. For Story it is the change in theme, merchandise and events and the 70%, price, quality and service, complements the experience. When you look at brands that are doing well like the clothing brand, J Crew, the surprise and delight factor that I've witnessed is that they are integrating more brand partnerships and developing new merchandise with old brands that we remember from our childhood. It's a surprising delight but also relevant."

Relevant and effective partnerships with brands such as Pepsi and General Electric are also an important factor to the Story business model.

"We look at our sponsors and partners not just as additional revenue streams, but as experts that add value to the conversations we're having and become the content. For example Benjamin Moore has much more authority in talking about Story colour; G.E. has a lot more authority in talking about manufacturing.

"Being a collaborative storyteller and having other people help us tell stories evokes a sense of curiosity because we are not coming from a place that says we know it all and we have all the answers, and I hope we never do. So, we bring in other people to help us tell stories, for example, Story New York was guest curated by Cool Hunting. We also work with different architects and interiors designers for every story."

The openness to community input is integral to the business and is what differentiates Story.

"The reality is that you can take those risks when you are not living, breathing and *dying by sales/square foot. This summer we had a lemonade stand in front of the store staffed by our young neighbors and you paid 25 cent for a cup. We have neighbors meeting each other for the first time and we see people so often that the sense of community is part of our DNA. We are also a community that appeals to men, women and children, all ages. For example, our pasta class had an 11 year old girl, a couple of 20 year olds on their first date, a 45 year old woman with her husband and a 58 year old woman who had just moved from London. The commonality was the experience.*

"There is something amazing that you can capture in real life that can be leveraged to impact online behaviour and we haven't even scratched the surface of creating these spaces. When you can seed a new product or take an existing product and work out how to innovate it, the store almost becomes the lab. We share insights with brands that can impact inventory planning, make marketing dollars and product development decisions more informed, and that is just the beginning – to me, that is the sexy part, the market research and capturing that data."

Rachel has created a multifaceted business model that is growing and developing all the time and refers to all that she has created with this new model of editorial and sponsorship as 'Retail Media.' An extension of that is that online sources can contribute to the store theme.

"For our G.E. Story Making Things, we partnered with Architizer, the largest online international community of architects. We did a competition that was called 'The Making of Making Things' and architects presented ideas with materials and Machines that would ultimately be part of the in store experience. This adds content to this story, creates exposure to an international community online and

ultimately it produced an innovative and dynamic store window and story."

It is the nature of this multidimensional model that makes Story stand out. Rachel's thinking is brought to life with a commitment to deliver something new to consumers, brands and to the retail industry.

"The reality is that the hottest commodity and the most luxurious item on the market

Courtesy of Story

right now is time. As people have less of it, they are smarter and more thoughtful with what they spend it on, how they spend it and where they spend it. We create environments where (in addition to shopping) you can learn new things and meet new people in a relevant way. If you tell a really good story through commerce and are thoughtful in creating a community through events, it can resonate with a wide range of people."

Prosperity

Caring about people
Establishing a legacy
Valuing what matters
Asserting influence

Caring about people

We care a lot about consumers. The US Federal Reserve, at the end of 2012, has blamed consumer uncertainty for pushing up the country's unemployment rate by 1 to 2%. In the UK, the Association of British Insurers is urging the government to align financial regulation more closely to what consumers want and need. In Singapore, a "Media Consumer Experience" study has revealed that the level of satisfaction among local consumers of media services is "relatively high". And New Zealand's media are fretting over a recent study indicating that consumer confidence is expected to remain fragile. Milton Friedman cared about consumers so much, he didn't even trust the government to protect them.

Business leaders also care about consumers. Steve Jobs proudly claimed that the Apple DNA "is as a consumer company",[100] while Thorsten Heins, upon his appointment at RIM, makers of Blackberry phones, committed to making the company "more consumer-oriented".[101] These consumers – whoever they are – must feel unbelievably loved and appreciated. But how many of us would seriously use the term "consumer" in a non-business context? How many of us would feel comfortable referring to our mothers as "consumers"? Do parents regard their children as consumers? Or as trainee consumers? How many of us would feel genuinely pleased to be openly referred to as a "consumer"? The term reduces us to a set of dollar signs. It's a remarkably dehumanising word to apply to people, and it's amazing how happy we are to read, hear and use it in the context of business.

Does any of this really matter or is this simply a matter of semantics? The business world is frequently guilty of introducing ugly and unnecessary words that seem designed to insult our intelligence. In 2011, Forbes magazine published a tongue-in-cheek glossary of the most annoying business jargon,[102] including words like "synergize" (which Big Bird of Sesame Street preferred to call "cooperate") and "utilize" (as opposed to the more sensible "use"). Arguably, the businesses that use this language provide a form of free entertainment: an opportunity for bloggers to take cheap shots at silly men in suits who have lost touch with reality. But the problem is this: nobody seems to be laughing. We don't even seem to question the use of the word "consumer" and everything it means.

In fact, the idea of the consumer is taken very seriously indeed. In the middle of a recession, we are frequently reminded of the importance of consumer sentiment to economic recovery. Consumer spending is seen as critical to economic growth. Businesses also take the idea seriously, going to great pains to measure and manage consumer satisfaction, loyalty and advocacy. Whether we're talking about economies, categories or individual businesses, it seems that growth requires consumption. At the level of the individual, our very happiness depends, evidently, on our continued ability to consume.

But people are capable of far more than simply spending money. "Consumer" is a limiting term. When businesses stop thinking of "consumers" and start thinking in terms of "people", they open themselves up to new opportunities for making friends and profiting from alternative sources of revenue. Many of us think of eBay as an online marketplace, but its founder, Pierre Omidyar, frequently emphasises the importance of people to his business, even though this is something he failed to appreciate in the early days of eBay. It started as an intellectual experiment to see if he could create an efficient marketplace on the internet. He was tinkering with technology. As the website started to grow at 20% to 30% each month and he started to receive feedback from its users, it dawned upon him that he had created more than a virtual marketplace: he had established a community of people. Trust is absolutely vital to eBay's ability to operate. In the words of its founder:

> What makes eBay successful – the real value and the real power at eBay – is the community. It's the buyers and sellers coming together and forming a marketplace. It's really this "of the people, by the people, for the people" environment. It's a very bottom-up environment. It's not the kind of approach that's top-down, centrally directed.

> There are 120 million people who are members of eBay, and over the last ten years, they've learned how to trust a complete stranger. eBay's business is based on enabling someone to do business with another person, and to do that, they first have to develop some measure of trust, either in the other person or the system. eBay's business could not have been successful unless it had that impact.

> We looked at that, and we said, "Heck, eBay can clearly have this impact, maybe there are other businesses and other

business models that can only be successful if they have a social impact." I think there's a potential for a lot of interesting business models that share with eBay the same principle.[103]

eBay helps us to see ourselves as more than just consumers: we can experience the pleasure of giving a good home to other people's unwanted bits and pieces; we can be paid not to throw away our old stuff by people who value it more than we do; we can participate as buyers, sellers and spectators within a community of peers. And in the process, we can take a step towards a sustainable model of consumption, complemented by refurbishment, repurposing, upcycling and recycling. Other businesses add a creative element to the principle alluded to above. Etsy has taken the essence of eBay and added a twist:

> Our mission is to empower people to change the way the global economy works. We see a world in which very-very small businesses have much-much more sway in shaping the economy, local living economies are thriving everywhere, and people value authorship and provenance as much as price and convenience. We are bringing heart to commerce and making the world more fair, more sustainable, and more fun.[104]

"eBay for the little guy" might be one way of describing Etsy, but it is anything but little. The business has over 19 million members and its 2011 sales were over US$525 million.[105] Although Etsy is an e-commerce website, there's something distinctly anti-consumer about a business that views its members as creators and appreciators of sustainability. It is a place for the "makers" of the world to meet and make friends with a sympathetic audience, who want to connect with a producer as well as a product.

Despite being digital businesses, eBay and Etsy arguably represent a return to a more intimate, participatory relationship between business and society. They demonstrate that the relationship between businesspeople and normal people doesn't have to be a zero-sum game. TomTom has established an online community to enable people to answer each other's questions about its products, to increase their technical knowledge and to solve each other's problems. In the first month of its establishment, this community dealt with 20,000 queries, saving the company an estimated US$150,000.[106]

So why would these people give up their free time to help solve strangers' problems with a device they aren't responsible for producing? Consumers are supposed to be self-interested, not altruistic. Actually, there are good reasons to think of consumers as selfish and mean. A recent experiment by psychologist Galen V. Bodenhausen[107] presented people with one of the following scenarios:

Four **individuals** (including you) must share a well during a water shortage.

Four **consumers** (including you) must share a well during a water shortage.

The study revealed that when people were labelled as "consumers", they were more likely than "individuals" to behave selfishly and they were less likely to trust other "consumers" to conserve water. It seems that consumers really are nastier than normal people. On the other hand, TomTom's "unsourced" support network shows that when we are given the opportunity, we tend to act like individuals rather than consumers.

Businesses need both employees and customers to thrive and survive, so why pretend otherwise?

There's another fundamental difficulty with businesses that call themselves "consumer-centric": the term implies that employees are only of secondary concern. The consumer comes first. Everybody else comes second. It seems absurd for a business to alienate employees this way. Businesses need both employees and customers to thrive and survive, so why pretend otherwise? Unilever CEO Paul Polman made the following observation in an interview with The Guardian newspaper:

> What people want in life is to be recognised, to be part of, to grow and to have made a difference. That difference can come in many forms; by touching someone, by helping others, by creating something that was not there before.[108]

Although these comments were made in response to a question about employees, it's significant that the emphasis is on people. Just as consumers are easy to caricature as selfish, mindless materialists, employees are easy to dismiss as insignificant cogs in a bigger machine. But as Paul Polman points out, employees are people too. This isn't a radical idea, but it can have radical implications. John Spedan Lewis had the very same idea in 1907, the year he was introduced as a partner in his father's department store empire. By 1914, he had fallen out with his father over his introduction of wacky initiatives designed to improve working conditions, such as reduced working hours and paid holidays. Nonetheless, he pushed ahead with his commitment to transforming his business from a company of employees to a community of people. In 1920, he introduced a staff council and a profit sharing scheme. In 1928, following his father's death, he assumed sole ownership of the company and almost instantly set about putting the business into the hands of the people who worked there. He created a Constitution and re-formed the company as a partnership between himself and all of his colleagues. The John Lewis Partnership was born. In an interview with the BBC in 1957, Spedan Lewis concluded with the following thoughts on the future of the partnership he had established:

> Rightly or wrongly I feel quite certain that the general idea of substituting partnership for exploiting employment is nowadays in the air and will spread through industry of all kinds. It is already dear to many hearts besides my own, for it makes work something to live for as well as something to live by. Here may be the new source of working energy of which our country is in such grave need.[109]

Nearly a century later, the sentiment expressed here is no less relevant. The subjects of work-life balance, staff motivation and worker exploitation remain stubbornly topical. Looking at business through a human lens – seeing people rather than consumers or employees – gives us the opportunity to ask fundamental questions about the role of business and its relationship to society: What does "better" working actually mean? How can businesses profit from people's creativity, empathy and intelligence to create growth for society, beyond simply paying for more stuff? And what role can businesses play in improving quality of life?

Caring about people | Pão de Açúcar

Pão de Açúcar
The enlightened retailer

Grupo Pão de Açúcar is on a mission to create a great shopping experience for its customers in Brazil and beyond. They are clearly doing something right. Since its establishment in the 1940s as the Pão de Açúcar pastry shop, the Group has grown to become Brazil's largest retailer, with over 1,800 supermarkets, hypermarkets, electronics stores, gas stations and drugstores.

So far so successful. But what's interesting about Pão de Açúcar is that this success is underpinned by a set of values that could best be described as exotic in the world of business. Not many companies count humility, emotional balance, determination and grit in their list of corporate values. These are oddly human characteristics for such a large corporation, particularly when so many of the Group's peers rely on an identikit set of values and behaviours.

Vitor Fagá, Pão de Açúcar's Executive Director of Corporate Relations, told us about the lengths that the Group is prepared to go to in its mission to create a great experience for its customers: *"We have a special department called "Casa do Cliente" (Customer's House). This department is physically separate from the company and is literally in a house. This department is in charge of making sure that the customer is satisfied. If not, Casa do Cliente will do everything possible to revert the situation or bring satisfaction to the customer. If customers have any complaints about the store, the products or services, the Casa do Cliente department will sort it out. We empower the department to allow them flexibility, influence and the ability to adjust*

processes at a store level to affect the customer in a positive way."

The customer is clearly an audience that Pão de Açúcar takes seriously. However, it would be wrong to think that the Group is willing to sacrifice the happiness and self-respect of its employees in a bid to please customers. Pão de Açúcar is better described as a people-focused organisation than a customer-focused business. Vitor Fagá explained to us that this focus on people is at the heart of the Group's success: *"We care in several dimensions: customers, employees, businesses and communities around our stores. We have been pushing the frontier of a pure retail supermarket or food retail chain to a more complex, dynamic and responsible company. We are a service company and one of the largest private employers in Brazil. So we take special care about people. This is key to our business. This is probably the key differentiator: to support our employees, not only in their daily work but also their family, health and any other dimensions. This is one our key goals as a company."*

When it comes to taking care of its employees, the Group is certainly prepared to put its money where its

Courtesy of Grupo Pão de Açúcar Press Relations

mouth is. Employees are offered a range of financial incentives to help improve their lives, from healthcare and dental plans to subsidised meals and discounts on hotels, theme parks and cultural events. The Group has also contributes 50% of tuition fees for every employee undergoing college education and offers scholarships to workers with physically or mentally impaired children. But Pão de Açúcar's employees aren't just supported, they are encouraged, recognised and rewarded for their contribution:

"Recognition goes beyond the financial. For example, we have a meeting every Monday morning with more than 200 company managers. In that meeting we introduce 3 or 4 people that deserve to be recognised by the company. We share their stories. And they are recognised in front of the 200 managers of the company. This is a small example; we keep them motivated not only in financial terms. That would be easy but we move ahead and do it in a different way,

we get them engaged and satisfied. When these employees go back to their store and tell other people, this keeps their team engaged and motivated."

This multiplier effect isn't restricted to Pão de Açúcar's role as an employer; the Group's scale means that it has an ability to positively influence the entire value chain in which it operates. Small suppliers aren't squashed like bugs. Quite the contrary. Pão de Açúcar established "Caras do Brasil" (Brazilian 'Face') a fair trade program that opens up its outlets to the trading of local products, with the aim of safeguarding biodiversity and local culture in the regions in which it operates.

"Caras do Brasil is a programme developed with small suppliers that usually create non-manufactured items such as, pots of honey, candy or towels. They typically don't have access to retail chains. We give them this access. We support them in many ways,

Caring about people | Pão de Açúcar

for example through advertising or by certifying their products. In some cases we support them financially. We created this programme 10 years ago and we have 160 products associated with it."

Beyond its own value chain, the Group embraces its ability to improve the long-term quality of life for Brazilian society at large. *"Sustainability for us is not a marketing action or topic, it is much more than that. Sustainability is the only way to do business right now and in the future. This cannot only be at an environmental level but also has to be at a social and economic level. For example, we support a specific institution (NATA) to provide training and education to communities. To train people to a professional level. We develop and educate people to be bakers, fishmongers and butchers. Usually we employ them in our stores, but if they want to open their own place they can. At the beginning we try to involve them in our stores, because it is the best way to gain experience."*

Despite the variety and scale of its activities in supporting Brazilian society, environment and economy, Vitor Fagá is extremely clear throughout our conversation that Pão de Açúcar is acting purely in its own interests. It's just that Pão de Açúcar's sense of self-interest happens to be far more enlightened than the average retailer. The Group plays many roles: maintaining human rights; contributing positively to society; promoting community wellbeing; safeguarding the environment; and working with partners and suppliers to meet the needs of its customers. All of these roles relates in some way to the company's DNA – the importance it places on people and its belief that long-term success relies on investing in their education, supporting their wellbeing and rewarding their achievements. *"Prosperity is definitely part of our mission, but we don't*

believe you can create prosperity alone. If you are not engaged with your employees, customers and society you will not be able to create prosperity in a sustainable and consistent way."

Caring about people | Pão de Açúcar

Courtesy of Grupo Pão de Açúcar Press Relations

Establishing a legacy

In his "Advice to a Young Tradesman", Benjamin Franklin counselled us to "Remember that time is money".[110] Ever since, business has felt like a race against the clock. In addition to managing people and processes, we also learn to manage time. We want to do as much as possible in as little time as possible. Time is a non-renewable resource. We spend it, borrow it and steal it. Making time is notoriously difficult, which is why we tend only to try to do this for our partners, our children, our friends or ourselves. Time is precious. We can't get it back. And each of us has only a limited amount of it to spend.

Students of economics are taught about the time value of money: the idea that money available now is more valuable than the promise of money in the future. If you were given a choice between receiving a hundred dollars today and a hundred dollars next year, you would be mad not to grab the money now. Even if you don't need the money until next year, you can place the hundred dollars in a savings account and have a hundred and one dollars in a year's time. And how much do you trust a promise to pay you a hundred dollars next year? You would have to know someone well enough to be confident that they'll remember and honour their promise. The time value of money is a core principle of finance and underpins many of the methods that are used to estimate the value of companies. It encourages us to discount the long-term and to place a premium on the short-term.

Economists and analysts discount the future because it is uncertain. The further into the future we go, the more uncertain it becomes and the more heavily we discount it. It's difficult enough to forecast revenue and profit a single year ahead, let alone five or ten years forward. Most financial forecasts stretch out between three and five years for this very reason. Beyond five years, the sheer amount of uncertainty involved makes prediction not only difficult but almost useless. Predicting what you'll have for lunch next Wednesday is tough. Predicting what will happen next year is infinitely tougher, which is why forecast data are so frequently revised. For example, in January 2012, the IMF published a revised set of estimates for world GDP growth in 2012. Included in these estimates was a prediction of growth in Europe. In September, the IMF had expected GDP in the Euro Area to grow by 1.1%. In December – only three months later – this estimate was revised to a contraction of -0.5%. This is a significant change of opinion after only three months. The point here is not to demonstrate that the IMF is poor at forecasting, but to show how hard it is to predict the future – and plan for it – without the help of a crystal ball.

But is the future something we plan for, or something we create for ourselves? Do we really need to be certain about the future before we can make decisions about long-term strategy?

The amount of uncertainty involved in long-range forecasting is either paralysing or liberating. In the former case, we are unable to make decisions about the long-term because we have insufficient data for those decisions to be considered reliable. In the latter case, in the absence of reliable data to tell us what to do, we'll just have to man up and make a decision anyway. Whether we like it or not, the decisions we make today have long-term implications. It seems silly to pretend that this isn't true, just because we can't reliably forecast those implications. Absence of evidence is not evidence of absence.

So how should we respond to uncertainty? Doing nothing is certainly an option. After all, the long-term is really just a series of short-terms. It's tempting to argue that as long as we keep things happy in the short-term, the long-term will resolve itself. But there are two big problems with this point of view. First of all, there are plenty of reasons to believe that life is going to get distinctly uncomfortable unless we start re-thinking how businesses work. While forecasting the future is difficult, we can at least extrapolate what happens if we continue to live, work, buy and die at current rates. The WWF established their One Planet Living Initiative in 2004 to highlight the stress that our current levels of consumption are placing on the planet's resources. The results of their analysis are a deeply troubling reminder that time might be a valuable resource, but so is the planet. And it seems we're running out of planets, as well as running out of time:

> Between 1961 and 2003, the impact of human activity on the planet's ecosystems increased by 150%. If current trends continue, by 2050 we will need a SECOND planet in order to be able to meet our demands for energy, water, food and shelter – and to absorb our wastes.[111]

More specifically, the average European lives as if there are three planets, while the average North American lives as if there are five planets. And this is one of the less alarming perspectives on the trouble that we're brewing. Doing nothing is no longer a viable option.

The second issue with a negative response to uncertainty is this: uncertainty is actually a good thing. Life is more interesting when we can't predict it. When we view uncertainty positively, we open ourselves up to possibility. Weekends are wonderful because we can decide what to do, who to see and where to go. The future is exciting because it is ours to create. Uncertainty is the mother of opportunity. The businesses that approach the future with a sense of optimism and a spirit of authorship will be those with the greatest potential to prosper.

IBM's Smarter Planet shows what can happen when a business takes the lead in authoring the future, shifting its focus from a narrow concept of value creation to a broader and more meaningful concept of prosperity. *The New York Times* recently described the initiative as "a bold and potentially lucrative experiment that could shape the future of cities around the world".[112] Through the initiative IBM applies its expertise in data analysis to help cities work more efficiently, coping with population growth, transport, pollution, crime, climate change and healthcare provision.

Uncertainty is actually a good thing. Life is more interesting when we can't predict it.

Making cities smart looks like it's going to be big business. The current global urban population is expected to double within one generation. According to the United Nations, the world's population will reach 8.3 billion by 2030 and 60% of these people will live in urban areas. Making cities smarter, safer and easier to navigate is going to play a major part in determining quality of life. Through their smarter cities initiative, IBM have established ground-breaking projects including a crime and safety control centre for New York, an integrated water management system in Iowa, a traffic prediction and management system in Singapore and an emergency response system for Rio de Janeiro. The company is now using the expertise and lessons gained through these partnerships to offer an "off-the-shelf" city management system to municipalities around the world. What we love about IBM's example is the enthusiasm with which it has risen to meet these challenges. Reflecting on her first six months as CEO at IBM, and her thousands of conversations with IBMers, Virginia Rometty was struck by the company's optimism about the future and its determination to play a significant role in its creation:

> First was the belief that despite the present troubles of the world's economy, the potential for a bright future, characterized by sustained prosperity and societal progress, is within our grasp. Second, I found a widespread belief that as IBM enters its second century, it possesses unique capabilities — in technology, in business expertise and most importantly, in a deep and systemic understanding of global citizenship — to lead the world in making that potential real. It is inspiring to hear that so many inside and outside the company believe it performs this distinctive role, and are eager to work together to see it succeed.[113]

Just as charity begins at home, so does the building of a brighter future. Magic Circle law firm Allen & Overy's Senior Partner David Morley made the following comment in the business' 2011 Annual Review:

In tough times it can be very tempting to focus on profitability and personal reward – the dollar today. But our partners recognise there's a longer game to be played and that they have a responsibility to pass on the firm in better shape than they found it.[114]

For this reason, the firm's leaders outline what they expect the business to look like in ten years' time – and how they are investing to create a healthy business in the long-term. The business has since introduced new working practices, such as "fluid resourcing" to allow the firm to cope with fluctuations in demand for its services. No aspect of the business has been neglected and the implications of innovative policies are considered from every angle: should the business buck the current fondness for large offices, which make a statement about its size and ambition, in favour of smaller hubs, which will allow for greater flexibility? Would moving to a network of hubs offer advantages other than cost savings? Would it allow people who work for Allen & Overy to achieve a better balance between work life and home life?

This people-centric approach shouldn't be remarkable or rare. But it is. It demonstrates that a business decision is no different from any other kind of decision. The human implications of each decision are carefully considered. For example, it is common in the legal profession to recruit graduates who are typically invited to become partners after ten to fifteen years of working their way up through the firm. This means that women in the business are invited to become partners around the same time that they are likely to start having children. So Allen & Overy offers part-time partnerships, as well as considering broader measures for creating flexible ways for people to develop their careers without sacrificing their personal ambitions. At the heart of these decisions is an incredibly simple idea: if you are interested in having a future, then it makes sense to think about it.

167

Arup
The key speech

Legacy is an extremely easy concept to associate with Arup. The company's 2011 Design Yearbook contains an exaltation of engineering feats: a self-sufficient, edible restaurant in Sydney; affordable kindergartens in Ghana; a particle accelerator in the USA; an observatory in Japan; and a tunnel linking Denmark and Germany.

Each project is staggering in scale and oozes ingenuity, artistry and longevity. But if you want to understand what legacy means within Arup, its Design Yearbook isn't the right document to look at.

On 9 July 1970, Ove Arup addressed a meeting of his international partners with what has come to be known as his 'Key Speech'. This speech is required reading for anybody who wants to understand what constitutes a cultural 'legacy' at Arup. In the speech, Arup describes his uncompromising ambition to make working at his company both interesting and rewarding. His ambition was to create an organisation that felt 'human and friendly, in spite of being large and efficient'. To this end, Arup expounded a set of 'aims', 'means', 'results' and 'principles' that could be used as a guide for future leaders of the business.

We spoke to one such leader, Tristram Carfrae, Arup's Head of Global Buildings Practice, who told us about the delicacy required to maintain the relevance of these ideals in a business that has grown dramatically over the 40 years since the Key Speech was delivered.
"We have no intention at the moment of refreshing the key speech. It is an authentic piece of writing by a man who studied philosophy before he studied engineering. The risk is whatever you write again wouldn't be anything like as good or as powerful as the authentic version that you have in front of you. However, you then have to treat it as a historical piece to some extent. But the bits that we perpetually refer to and people come to love are the values in the key speech, if I can call them that, which he refers to as being the aims, the means and the results. They are the reasons why people come to join Arup. And they are things that we live and breathe every day."

Even 40 years on, Ove Arup's ideal of a 'humane' organisation informs how today's leaders measure their own success. As Carfrae explains, *"In Ove's Speech, he states that being a humane organisation is an aim. In most organisations this would be a means. It would be something to have as a chassis to help you achieve something else. For me it is vitally important that for Arup it is part of the objective itself. The other [important aspect of the speech] is money. Ove says that money can be divisive, but at the same time, it is essential. It is a means. You have to be solvent. So money has this black and white aspect. It is absolutely fundamental to existence. At the same time, making tonnes of it is not an ambition. In the hurly burly of business, most of the people that you work with and for — most of the*

Photograph by Godfrey Argent, courtesy of Arup

Establishing a legacy | Arup

Courtesy of Arup

stuff you read in the newspapers — is actually all about maximising the monetary gain of an organisation. So you have to take the time to reflect: what do you actually want the money for?"

This question is more profound within Arup than many businesses. Arup is a wholly independent organisation owned in trust for the benefit of its employees and their dependents. Without external shareholders or investors, the question of money becomes a question of sustainability: how much money does an organisation require to safeguard its future? And what will that future look like? Arup must reach its own conclusions independently. This independence is central to Arup's ability to adhere to its founder's ideals. *"Something our clients don't always seem to think is important to them is the idea of independence: the independence that comes from owning ourselves and that gives us freedom to think. "It takes away the pressure of having to*

owe something to an owner external to yourselves. Instead it gives you a fantastic opportunity to think about the real issues on behalf of the client. To really challenge and question. To ask the question, "why?" which is difficult with some clients. They are not expecting the people they have employed to ask, "why?" The most difficult attribute to persuade clients as having a real benefit is the idea of independence."

Its independence enables Arup to think seriously about the long-term. To set out a vision for the future and to invest in making it happen. While many businesses may measure their legacy in terms of scale — number of employees, customers served, markets covered, annual revenues, market capitalisation or profit — Arup's focus remains steadfastly on the quality and permanence of its work. Even to the company responsible for some of the world's most imposing structures, bigger does not always mean better. *"At the moment there are a huge amount of*

Courtesy of Arup

Courtesy of Arup

acquisitions in our sector. A lot of firms are becoming very large. Sometimes we feel like we are sitting in a rowing boat in the middle of the ocean with big oil tankers passing us by. But we always decide when we think about it that we don't want to be an oil tanker. As you grow, you inevitably become more ordinary. The more people you put in a room, the more likely the IQ will average at 100. So [we focus on how to] remain distinctive, remain what we are, remain empowering. How do we address the world's needs? How do we remain cohesive? We think that means remaining true to our foundation and values, as illustrated in the Key Speech."

The Key Speech, married with Arup's independent status, ensures that the company will never stray too far from its roots, will never lose sight of what makes it special. When we ask of any bold plans for the future, the response is characteristically defiant: *"It's not going to be terribly exciting. Just more of the same thing. It's a dull answer but we deliberately change slowly."* If all companies were as dull as Arup, the world might be a more enjoyable place in which to work.

Valuing what matters

We don't like to talk of "creativity" and "accounting" in the same breath. This dredges up memories of corporate fraud, paper shredders and financial scandal. We prefer to think of accountancy in terms of conformity: a sober group of reliable people diligently adhering to a strict set of legal and ethical principles. The language of accountancy encourages this image of prudence. Sheets are balanced, as opposed to dynamic. Expenses can be abnormal, whereas revenue can be anticipated. Debt can be bad, but is rarely desired. When it comes to measuring business success, reliability, predictability and comparability trump innovation and change. We usually like accountants to be boring.

But contrary to popular belief, accountants can be a creative group of people. Lionel Richie is an accountant-musician. So is Kenny G. John Grisham is an accountant-novelist. Walter Diemer — also an accountant — will go down in history as the inventor of "Dubble Bubble" bubble gum. It seems a shame that accountants have to resort to saxophony, inventing bubble gum and recording platinum albums as an outlet for their creativity. Particularly when the way we measure business performance is in dire need of innovation. Accountancy rules have struggled to keep pace with the changing sources of corporate value.

The accountancy world spent much of the nineties and noughties debating how best to respond to the increasing importance of intellectual property, such as knowhow and brands. Even after decades of debate, accounting for intangible assets remains a notoriously thorny subject. The focus of conversation has now moved on to the even more challenging issue of how businesses can establish a more holistic statement of the health of their business. This means journeying even further into the world of the unmeasured, into areas such as making people happy, contributing to cultural development and preserving the planet.

This conversation is forcing us to consider more deeply why businesses exist in the first place: you can't create a meaningful system for measuring success unless you first define what success actually means.

Let's start with a simple definition: success in business is about finding new ways to do more with less. This is an often repeated and much maligned idea, largely because it is typically introduced by managers to justify lay-offs to an already demoralised workforce and to explain why workers who survive the cull will now have to work longer hours for lower pay. But "do more with less" doesn't have to mean "stop complaining and get back to work". It doesn't have to mean cutting costs or cutting corners. John Elkington isn't an accountant, but he is responsible for reframing the idea of "doing more with less" in more positive, meaningful terms. He coined the term "triple bottom line" to suggest a bigger concept of value, encompassing the economic, environmental and social impact of business. Forward-thinking businesses are beginning to adopt these ideas to create greater transparency and accountability.

Natura is Brazil's largest beauty and wellbeing company, established in Sao Paolo in 1969. The company is explicit in its belief that the value and longevity of business is "connected to its ability to contribute to the evolution of society and its sustainable development". These are more than just words. Natura has embedded social, economic and environmental concerns in what it calls an "integrated management culture". Through a combination of hard and soft measures, each of these categories affects how managers and their decisions are appraised.

The company's profit share system takes all of the dimensions of the triple bottom line into account, including EBITDA, employee loyalty, feedback from the organisational climate survey, carbon emissions and inventory management. This focus on a broader definition of value creation hasn't come at the expense of growth – quite the opposite. Between 2007 and 2011, net revenue increased from R$3 billion to R$5 billion and EBITDA doubled from R$700 million to R$1.4 billion in the same period.[115] In the company's own words, Natura has demonstrated "that a company does not have to make trade-offs between doing good and doing well".

...high sustainability companies are fundamentally different from their traditional counterparts

This is a trade-off many of us assume is an in-built feature of business. On the one hand, sensational stories about executive bonuses, banker blowouts and employee burnouts encourage the belief that profits are the result of exploitation of people, consumers or natural resources. On the other hand, "doing good" has traditionally been seen as the role of NGOs, charities and philanthropists: turning a profit by doing good is almost seen as a form of moral bankruptcy. For others of us, this is an issue of credibility, as demonstrated by the following comments made by Professor Aneel Karnani, one of the most vocal opponents of social enterprise, in a 2010 interview with the "Beyond Profit" e-magazine:

> I think the concept of social business is either an oxymoron or a somewhat confused concept. If it's a business, and it earns not only enough revenue to cover its costs, but also enough to cover the cost of capital, then it's a good business. That's the whole point of capitalism, that business has social value and increases social welfare at the same time. So every business is social. On the other hand, if you don't

make money, then you're not a business. You could be doing something that is socially useful – this is what NGOs have always done – but then I don't see why we should call it a social business.[116]

To be perfectly honest, we understand the scepticism. Examples of businesses like Natura seem few and far between. Intuitively, it feels fair to assume that tree-hugging is not a profitable way for any business manager to spend his or her time. Fortunately, our intuition doesn't count for very much. A recent study[117] by Robert Eccles, Ioannis Ioannou and George Serafeim of Harvard Business School compared the performance of ninety high sustainability companies with ninety low sustainability companies.

Accountancy rules have struggled to keep pace with the changing sources of corporate value.

The authors of the study demonstrate that high sustainability companies are fundamentally different from their traditional counterparts. They are more likely to include soft measures of environmental and social performance in determining executive compensation. They are more likely to engage a broader group of stakeholders in decision-making. They have an investor base with longer-term perspectives and they discuss long-term measures of success in investor calls. They are also more transparent, disclosing a greater level of non-financial information about employees, customers and suppliers. So rather than being distracted, it seems that companies with sustainable cultures are actually managed using a broader set of measures, with a greater level of dialogue and more open disclosure. Some people might call this "being more professional".

But are companies who put sustainability at the core of their business more profitable? The authors tracked company performance of the two groups between 1993 and 2010, examining stock market as well as accounting performance. In terms of stock market performance, the high sustainability portfolio significantly outperformed the low sustainability group. Investing US$1 in the high sustainability portfolio in 1993 would have yielded US$22.6 in 2010. In comparison, investing the same amount in the low sustainability portfolio would have yielded US$15.4 – nearly a third less. In terms of accounting performance, the study revealed that high sustainability companies not only offered significantly higher returns than their low sustainability counterparts, but they did so with significantly lower volatility. In other words, sustainable companies generate significantly higher returns for significantly lower risk.

...a company does not have to make trade-offs between doing good and doing well.

The Harvard study seems to point to a new reality: that sustainability is part and parcel of managing a business professionally and profitably. Changing the way we think about value, as well as how we measure it, will be a slow and difficult process. Measuring profit alone is hard enough. Developing reliable financial measures of a business' social and environmental impact is even tougher. There are no easy answers and it's unlikely that there will ever be a "perfect" approach to measuring the broader impact of business. But this isn't about trying to place a price tag on people or nature. The companies included in the Harvard study – Natura included – use a combination of soft measures as well as hard measures, non-financial as well as financial. Adopting a broader concept of value is more about creativity than calculators.

Valuing what matters | EGG-energy

EGG-energy:
Cracking the power supply in Tanzania

Energy in sub-Saharan Africa is an interesting subject, and one that a small group of Engineering PhDs and MBAs from MIT and Harvard wanted to explore more. They looked at what kind of businesses would be useful in a place like Tanzania, where only a small percentage of the rural population have access to electricity.

Photograph by Eric Persha, courtesy of EGG-energy

EGG-energy is a 'for profit' business, with a social mission — they believe in the potential for private enterprise to empower its customers, but they have a commitment to the social goal of cheap, clean power for the developing world. In Tanzania, government funds aren't available for the extension of the power grid to villages and homes; individual customers would have to pay the upfront

cost (in the region of several thousands of dollars) to extend the grid, meaning that at the moment, the cost is just too high. So here was an alternative approach.

The young team developed a business model and pricing scheme that allows profit sharing between the end user (35% annual savings on their energy expenditures), local entrepreneurs

Valuing what matters | EGG-energy

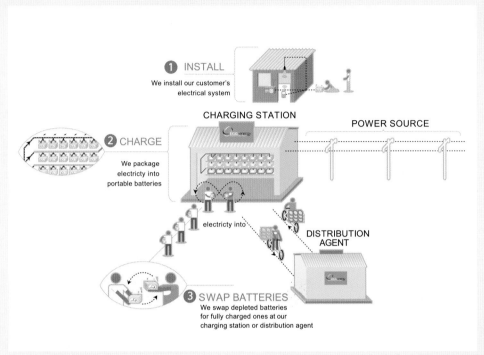

Courtesy of EGG-energy

(6-year average profit of 24%) and EGG-energy (internal rate of return of 27% over six years).

EGG-energy took a year to work on the business plan and raise funds, and one of their biggest lessons was that they couldn't rely on word of mouth to spread the message about their service. After three months, they noticed that customer recruitment was still slow, so they developed a sales strategy, including a local sales force to visit communities with kits to explain the value and the savings of the service.

We spoke to Jamie Yang, CEO of EGG-energy, who told us *"We noticed there were a lot of people who were living close to a power source, especially the grid, and yet had no access to energy from the grid and little hope of that happening. We saw that the last mile of delivery of energy was broken and there seemed to be an easy way to fix it. Or at least to create a temporary solution that would allow people to improve what they were doing and save money in the meantime."*

The idea is very simple — take power at its source (a grid connection or a renewable electricity generation plant) and package it in small, transportable, rechargeable batteries. EGG-energy uses a 12V 12Ah deep-cycle sealed lead acid battery that can power lights, a radio, and mobile phones for a household for about five nights in a typical household. The batteries are owned and maintained by EGG-energy, and rented to customers for a subscription fee. Customers can change their depleted batteries for a fully charged one at any time at a number of charging stations. At the end of their useful life, batteries are removed from circulation and recycled.

The main component in EGG-energy's 'portable grid' is the battery — they realised that they needed to be small and light, easy to transport and rugged so that they don't break or spill during transportation. EGG-energy uses battery technology invented for use in airplanes, so that they are light and tough, and can be carried in a single hand. EGG-energy take their service right into the home; when a customer subscribes, a trained technician will install the necessary wiring to make sure the batteries are easy to use and effective, as well as safe.

The intention has been to replace other temporary sources of energy, like kerosene and AA batteries. The light from a kerosene lamp is less than 5% of an incandescent bulb and these lamps are a major contributor to indoor air pollution and respiratory problems, especially among women and girls. The batteries are much more efficient in providing light and power, and a lot kinder to the environment. The local feedback is that a large proportion of EGG-energy's customers don't use kerosene any more.

The effect on everyday life for EGG-energy users has been life changing, and Jamie Yang told us *"Our lights have been important in helping kids to study at night. It is a story that people really like to hear. But the lights have been important in other ways too, like social gatherings, allowing people to gather after sunset around the house and be able to see each other's faces. Being able to get around the house, providing extra security, things like that are a major improvement to people's lives."*

In a wider sense, EGG-energy is investing in the local economy, recruiting local people, and intending to develop and train their employees. Only three of the staff are expats, the rest are Tanzanian. It's an important part of EGG-energy's development to listen to their employees, and to understand where they're coming from. This is what gives EGG-energy a better understanding of how business transactions are done, and how people understand and use their services. They rely on their staff to keep them up to date with local information and intelligence.

In taking on local people, Jamie says *"We look to hire more for attitude and are willing to invest in the development and training of people. We look for an entrepreneurial attitude. We're trying to structure the stations in ways that the leader of that station feels a sense of ownership and treats it like their own business."*

Most of the training and development for technicians starts with the simple household battery systems and technical training, but EGG-energy are working on developing sales and managerial training and capabilities for their teams.

The question of infrastructure is a big one in the setup and development of EGG-energy. It's important that there is a robust supply chain, and the business understood the importance of local entrepreneurs and businesses in this chain. They partner with local dukas (the Tanzanian version of convenience stores) and delivery businesses for pick-up and drop-off services for the batteries. Piggy-backing on what is already there, using local resources and supporting local businesses are key to their success and development.

What is clear, at the core of the business, is a strong commitment to valuing what matters: *"We're looking for ways to improve our customers' lives and if our activities are doing something other than that then it doesn't really fall within what the mission of the company is."*

Valuing what matters | EGG-energy

As for the future, the plan is *"to get everyone on a modern electricity grid. This is a good solution for now and it allows us to start building some infrastructure towards what could eventually be a very smart distributed electricity grid".*

In Tanzania, EGG-energy is improving quality of life, providing accessible, affordable and sustainable sources of power – perhaps they have cracked it after all.

Photographs by Eric Persha, courtesy of EGG-energy

Asserting influence

Capitalism has cogs. Businesses have levers. And dashboards. And gears. And silos. Making things happen in business is a matter of knowing which buttons to push. In this context, asserting influence feels like something of a dark art: manipulating employees, suppliers and consumers to create competitive advantage. But the popularity of this mechanistic view of business seems to be dwindling. The simple mechanisms of supply and demand are being replaced by a more complex view of business as a system – or an ecosystem – in which businesses are part of a community. Competition still exists, but success also depends on a business' ability to co-operate, to connect and to contribute to the integrity of the system as a whole.

The World Resources Institute describes ecosystems as 'the productive engines of the planet".[118] This description seems as relevant to businesses as it does to grasslands and forests. Where machines are solid, precise and in constant need of maintenance, ecosystems are dynamic, self-sustaining and diverse. Business is rarely ordered and predictable – it's messy and exuberant. Making sense of this messiness involves negotiating a complex system of people and problems to create opportunity. Being a leader in business can mean one of two things: acting alone to achieve dominance over this messy system or stimulating people to act together to improve the system as a whole.

Leaders stand apart, but not alone.

Many businesses are keen to communicate their leadership ambitions. Deutsche Bank likes to talk about leadership in its corporate mission statement: 'We compete to be the leading global provider of financial solutions, creating lasting value for our clients, our shareholders, our people and the communities in which we operate".[119] Despite the mention of communities, this statement is more about domination. The bank's primary function is to compete, to provide and to create.

PUMA is another German business that likes to talk about leadership, but in a very different sense: "At PUMA, we believe that our position as the creative leader in Sportlifestyle gives us the opportunity and the responsibility to contribute to a better world for the generations to come."[120] The emphasis here positions PUMA as a contributor rather than sole creator of change. In 2011, the company released its first Environmental Profit & Loss Account (EPL) for the previous calendar year. PUMA's EPL is a compelling demonstration of creative accounting in its most positive sense. One of the more striking aspects of the EPL is that it doesn't consider the company in isolation, but as part of a broader business ecosystem. According to the report, PUMA's direct impact on the environment is around €8 million – the notional cost to the planet of PUMA's offices, warehouses and stores in 2010. But once the company considers the impact of its entire supply chain, this figure spirals to €137 million. In his foreword to the EPL, Jochen Zeitz, Executive Chairman of PUMA and Chief Sustainability Officer of PPR, highlighted the importance of PUMA's ability to influence other companies in its supply chain:

Business is rarely ordered and predictable – it's messy and exuberant.

So if PUMA is to successfully reduce its environmental impact, we have to address the activities of our supply chain partners that generate 94% of our total environmental impact. While we recognize that this is our responsibility, it is at the same time the responsibility of numerous other companies. In order to make a real change we, along with our industry peers, have to collaborate and work responsibly to help reduce the impacts of external supplier factories and raw material producers at least to a point where nature can recover rather than being depleted further, resulting in environmental damages that cannot be undone.

This isn't a case of passing the buck. PUMA understands that it is part of a larger system and has chosen to take the lead in tackling an issue that threatens the future of the system in which it operates. In doing so, PUMA isn't chasing some bizarre dream of global domination, but is seeking to make a meaningful contribution to the welfare of its customers, partners and the communities it relies upon for its profits. Leading a group of businesses to create change is a far greater challenge than acting alone. Since publishing the EPA, PUMA has been tackling this challenge in digestible pieces. For example, in April 2010 PUMA commissioned a lifecycle assessment of its shoe packaging. The report found that user behaviour had a significant impact on the environmental performance of its shoe packaging – particularly since 90% of people carry shoe boxes home in a carrier bag.[121]

As a result, the company decided that the shoebox of the future wouldn't be a box at all, but a bag – a 'Clever Little Bag' made from recycled polypropylene, which people can carry without an additional carrier bag. The Clever Little Bag uses 65% less cardboard than a standard shoebox, saving 8,500 tonnes of paper and 1 million litres of water each year, but more significant is that it doesn't require us to use an additional bag. And we no longer need to fill our garages and attics with mountains of unwanted shoeboxes. PUMA isn't alone in interpreting leadership as a collective phenomenon. Since its establishment in 1921, Alessi has established itself as one of the world's most prominent design companies: according to its website, Alessi products are part of more permanent museum collections than any other design company. It's not difficult to understand why. Alessi has produced citrus squeezers that resemble alien spaceships, analogue watches without hands and conical kettles. The company has worked with over 500 designers, artists and architects such as Salvador Dali, Philippe Starck, Zaha Hadid and Ettore Sottsass, not to mention businesses such as Seiko, Fiat, Siemens and Philips. As a result of this collaborative approach to design, Alessi has extended its influence from housewares to watches, textiles, phones and cars.

Behind these collaborations is a simple mission: to make everyday objects spectacular. In doing so, Alessi creates products that are designed to endure. Even the humble citrus squeezer is designed to be something you want to keep for the rest of your life. This is in stark contrast to the recent policy of planned obsolescence and the culture of semi-disposability peddled by mobile handset manufacturers, the car industry and the (fast) fashion industry. Alessi shows that leadership requires a group. Strong reputations allow businesses to attract talent and to bring together dream teams of collaborators. We are culturally richer as a result.

This is what true leadership in business is about. Leaders stand apart, but not alone. The ability to influence rests upon a willingness to see beyond the four walls of our own business, to demonstrate a willingness to engage with the world and to make it better.

Asserting influence | BMWi

BMWi
New questions, new answers

The automotive industry is at a crossroads. The price of fuel is likely to rise over the coming decades, potentially pricing many people out of car ownership. Governments are tightening their stance towards emissions. And a new generation of megacity dwellers is emerging, characterised by a reduced need for private transport and a mounting apathy toward car ownership.

© BMW AG

This is the kind of situation that might prompt some car manufacturers either to bury their heads in the sand or else to head for the hills. But at BMW, it has prompted a fundamental questioning of their company's future: if individual mobility is going to be viable in 2020, how can BMW turn these challenges into opportunities for increasing its influence? In 2007 BMW's Chief Executive, Norbert Reithofer, established 'project i' to develop 'sustainable and visionary' concepts for mobility. The project was set up as an internal think tank of eight people, with Ulrich Kranz at its head. The project team was handed a blank sheet of paper and initially worked outside the normal company structure to create an aspirational vision for the future of BMW. This is one of the most striking aspects of the project: in the beginning, there were no preconceptions about the solution. There was simply a very big question to consider. As Mr Kranz explained to us:

"We started thinking about what the future might look like. We went to big cities all over the world and interviewed potential customers. Some of the team lived with them in their homes for a couple of days.

a vision for the future of mobility. As the project gained momentum, the team extended its influence through dialogue with other parts of the company, drawing on the talent and experience across BMW Group.

"People need to have the freedom to think outside the box otherwise you are sitting inside an existing system and plans. I took the team from all the divisions of BMW, we had production guys, architects, designers, purchasing guys, logistics, finance and some planners. We sat together and we thought, "Who do we need for the next

© BMW AG

We drove with them in their cars. We also interviewed mayors and city planners because we wanted to know their requirements concerning the future."

The 'project i' team reviewed over 300 global trends and through this combination of insight and foresight established

couple of months to work together and to prove if these things are possible?"
The good thing is that we have lots of smart engineers in the company. My colleagues in the other product areas watch us closely. They look at what kind of technology is developed in 'project i' and what they can use. I am convinced that you will see the

© BMW AG

BMWi technology in other company brands."

In 2010, these 'smart engineers' were joined by Benoit Jacob, 'project i's Head of Design. Although his background is in car design, it was clear from the outset that his task was to develop far more than just a new car. BMWi's aim is to design a completely new set of behaviours.

"Our job is to create emotion. Our job is essentially to create desirability. To combine desirability and efficiency. Responsibility and sustainability. There's little point making something highly efficient if the world doesn't want it. BMW is well positioned to convince the world that sustainability and responsibility can be combined with attraction, beauty and sexiness. Not as a few statements on a piece of paper but to actually turn [sustainability] into an experience, and an experience that is great."

'project i' is more than BMW's response to a changing future: it is a clear statement that the company intends to take responsibility for authoring a more desirable, more sustainable world for future generations. It's staggering to see how much has been accomplished in just five years. BMW has set up an entire value chain from scratch. The body of the vehicle is spun from carbon fibre produced in a purpose-built facility powered by a hydro-electric plant. The BMWi plant in Leipzig is powered entirely by renewable energy. BMW has set up a venture capital company in New York to invest in a broader set of mobility services that will create an entire ecosystem around BMWi and extend the company's influence far beyond the role of a traditional car manufacturer. These services include a network of charging points, an online marketplace for parking spaces and smartphone apps that deliver location-based mobility services. Uli Kranz calls this a '360' approach.

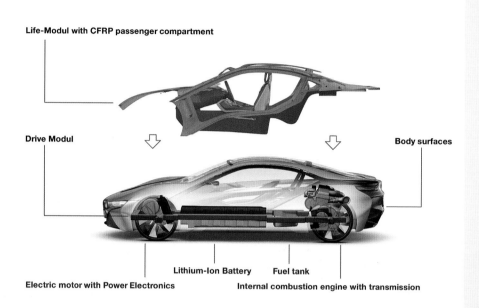

Life-Modul with CFRP passenger compartment

Drive Modul

Body surfaces

Lithium-Ion Battery   **Fuel tank**

Electric motor with Power Electronics   **Internal combustion engine with transmission**

© BMW AG

"What was clear in every market is that users want a connection to public transport. They want communication between their car and telephone, so they always know the state of charge and how far they can go. These are the mobility solutions that customers expect from us and these are the things we are going to introduce, or that we have already introduced – for example 'Drive now', the premium car sharing service, and other solutions. We are going to give them access to public charging spots. We are going to check their house: what kind of charging speed is available? What kind of infrastructure do they have to install?"

"What we learned pretty early on is that we have to offer more than just zero emission vehicles. This is what we call the 360 approach. We have a complete 360 package available when we hand over the vehicle. This is just the start. There is more to come.

As soon as there are more electric vehicles we will see more opportunities. We are doing more than just bringing an electric vehicle into the market. We are 100% convinced that this kind of vehicle and the 360 approach that we are offering is new and there are customers out there who will appreciate it."

BMWi is a remarkably pure vision, not just of BMW's future but all of our futures. Nothing was compromised in the achievement of this vision. Everybody involved in the project is extremely clear on this point. BMWi has to deliver 'pure driving pleasure'. It has to reflect the company's DNA. It has to build on the business' rich heritage. It has to demonstrate what the company understands by 'next premium'. The story of BMWi encompasses many of the themes discussed in this book. Establishing a vision with integrity. Demonstrating curiosity about the future.

© BMW AG

Crafting an entire ecosystem. Developing elegant solutions to enormously complex problems. Time will tell whether prosperity ensues. What we can say for certain is that BMWi demonstrates what is possible when a company takes its future seriously.

Given how many companies struggle with the issue of business model innovation, BMW's approach is remarkably straightforward: set up an internal think tank, give it a problem to solve and then assimilate what you've learned into the wider organisation. In Benoit Jacob's words, *"New questions are likely to generate new answers."* All you need is a blank sheet of paper and the right combination of imagination, dialogue, investment and ingenuity. Everything else is just an excuse. Ulrich Kranz summed this up in his parting comment to us: *"It is not rocket science — if you have the right people, motivation and support."*

Afterword on Prosperity

by Jonathon Porritt
Forum for the Future

There are good reasons to be fairly upbeat about the way in which some of today's more sustainable businesses are starting to redefine what we mean by prosperity. As this chapter demonstrates, there is now a tonne of evidence to demonstrate that more sustainable enterprises are, on average, more profitable and less vulnerable to market volatility than less sustainable enterprises. That's even got conventional market analysts recalibrating their assumptions about what we mean by business success.

However, that by itself is clearly not sufficient if we are intent on bringing about a much more radical "re-humanisation" of business, as is argued in this book. Many of today's best-known sustainability success stories are still basing that success on completely conventional measures of profit, Return on Capital Employed, and so on. The "unmeasurables" (as they are described in this book) are often of secondary importance; the iron-clad orthodoxies of business management, with all its pseudo-scientific mumbo-jumbo, are still just as prevalent as they've been over the last few decades.

The hypothesis in this book is that these orthodoxies are still dominant because of the way we've come to "frame" the business of business. The pursuit of profit has been imbued with a canonical authority; competitiveness (of the "winner-takes-all" variety) is interpreted as a non-negotiable requirement for business success; and we as "citizens" have been recast as an undifferentiated collective of consumers, just as nature has been recast as a soulless store of resources or natural assets.

Business schools mindlessly amplify this framing of business today. Politicians feel more and more comfortable co-opting its precepts into their own political worldviews – as in Tony Blair's infamous reduction of his country into "UK plc". Michael Sandel has elegantly revealed the creeping "marketisation" of institutions and transactions in societies that once drew on the full breadth of human relationships rather than the simple exchange of a monetised service.

This debate about the nature of business is therefore a proxy for a much bigger debate about the nature of human nature. A more holistic, creative vision of business is always going to struggle in a world where people are represented primarily as atomised, narrowly self-interested individuals, driven first and foremost by the prospect of short-term personal gain. We need to see people differently for business to prosper intelligently.

For me, that's what comes through most strongly in these stories – for let us not call them "case studies"! When Bill Gore talks about making money as "a creative activity", what he's really demonstrating is a self-fulfilling trust in human nature to work collaboratively and respectfully in the interest of something bigger than the individual standing alone.

But it isn't easy. These inspirational stories and characters are all too obviously working against the grain of what passes for normal in today's world.

Just as today's "epidemic of obesity" can be attributed primarily to the self-reinforcing mechanisms of an "obesogenic environment" (i.e. an environment that plays so seductively on those behaviours and desires that lead to obesity), so today's prevailing self-interest can be attributed to the self-reinforcing mechanisms of an "egogenic environment" – in other words, an environment that affirms, reinforces and positively rewards people putting self-interest before all else. Mrs Thatcher's somewhat apocryphal statement that "there is no such thing as society" has become the poster child for at least three decades' worth of ideological crusading that have triumphed the rights and claims of individualism at the expense of community and planet.

This explains why progressive businesses today are doing something more than running their own business on a more progressive and sustainable basis. They are part of a much larger groundswell reclaiming what it is to be a fully-functioning, connected human being, instinctively and empathetically taking into account the interests of others (including the interests of future generations) as well as the interests of self.

These inspirational stories and characters are all too obviously working against the grain of what passes for normal in today's world.

There's a nice irony here too. Some of the businesses most actively helping to redefine business in those terms are wholly internet-based with zero face-to-face contact. Companies like eBay and Etsy thrive by creating communities of citizens rather than mailing lists of consumers. These virtual, dis-intermediated businesses (with most of the "middle men" cut out of the value chain) have been able to create a platform for more intimate, participatory relationships than many "bricks and mortar" companies.

As the authors put it:

> eBay helps us to see ourselves as more than just consumers: we can experience the pleasure of giving a good home to other people's unwanted bits and pieces; we can be paid not to throw away our old stuff by people who value it more than we do. We can participate as buyers, sellers and spectators within a community of peers.

In that regard, there's no doubt that some of today's most dynamic peer-to-peer companies are blazing a trail for much more collaborative, less impactful patterns of consumption.

And the same is true of leading companies like Unilever (whose CEO, Paul Polman, is intent on investing the Unilever brand — as well as many of its individual product brands — with a raft of qualities that consumers can intuitively relate to) and Nike, who use innovation and collaborative working (harnessing the energy of "citizen influencers") to change the nature of consumption.

Unfortunately, this is not exactly the easiest of times to be accelerating this benign and inspiring recalibration of the business of business. Uncertainty may indeed be "the mother of opportunity", as the authors claim, but it also provides the justification for backward-looking, risk-averse responses from politicians to the state of the world today.

Against an unremittingly gloomy backdrop of debt, spending cuts and very high levels of unemployment (particularly amongst young people), all that governments seem prepared to do is to find a path back to the same old life-destroying model of economic growth that got us into such trouble in the first place. At the same time, mainstream investors breathe in that toxic mix of political desperation and retrospection, remaining faithful to their old investment orthodoxies in a way that stifles any prospect for a more profound transformation of this irretrievably broken model of capitalism.

We just need to be mindful of those structural blockages. After all, it's nearly eighty years since John Spedan Lewis allowed himself to dream a little about exactly that kind of transformation:

> Rightly or wrongly, I feel quite certain that the general idea of substituting partnership for exploiting employment is nowadays in the air, and will spread through industry of all kinds. It is already dear to many hearts besides my own, for it makes work something to live for as well as something to live by. Here may be the new source of working energy of which the world is in such grave need.

And we're still in need of it today. Which is all the more reason to celebrate the extraordinary achievements of those who've created strong and beautiful businesses that fly (like wild ducks!) in the face of all those who would keep stripping business back to the sole goal of profit maximisation on a planet that seems to be rapidly imploding.

Conclusion

"It's far better to buy a wonderful company at a fair price than a fair company at a wonderful price."

Warren Buffett in a letter to investors 1989

Business always will be a human story. Yet business is sometimes allowed to be the bully at the head of the table – to become boorish, one-dimensional and not at all the person it really is. It may be because there are too many facts, too much data and not enough balance leading to a lack of corporate awareness of the other important characteristics we examine in Business is Beautiful.

If this book achieves anything it will be these two things: One, it will help remind us (through the examples of those great businesses who have taken part in Business is Beautiful) that standing apart is easier when businesses behave like people, and value what people really want to value. A graspable meaning, not necessarily articulated in a written vision, but an unselfconscious purpose. And two, that behaving this way is, strangely, the best way in which to keep on having good ideas, without which no business has much chance of staying in the game long term.

Our ideas may come across as a challenge, and the businesses that we chose to feature may be controversial. But to us it proves there isn't a pure argument to be made in business, a reason why business remains fascinating for both its mechanical and, more lastingly, its human qualities. Take the unarguably successful business record of Warren Buffett – a record you might think was enough to satisfy anyone. But while there is great interest in his business deals, there is as much written about Warren Buffett the man, his family, how and why such an exceptional person came to be the way he is, as about his business empire. Proof again that the human story is the story.

When we think about ourselves in business, we somehow cannot quite remember the things we spend most of our time talking about in meetings. We see this in the kind of government committees prevalent today — business people are hauled up in front of politicians to answer difficult questions about details they are asked to recall from their working week. Strangely in most cases, they don't remember much. In some cases this can be just bending the truth, to protest a lack of memory, but it is true that we tend to be able to remember the human elements that connect and enliven the otherwise anodyne parts of business life.

For example, a former colleague of ours, an exceptionally sensitive and intelligent man, found himself presenting to a board, in a typical boardroom situation. As he launched off those first few sentences designed to establish his credibility he noticed in his peripheral vision two men, one passing a small piece of folded paper to the other and the other opening it, reading the short text written inside and then smirking with a nod back to his neighbour and the paper pushed beside him. On seeing this a jolt of self-consciousness shot through our speaker who became increasingly convinced that the note had described him in a negative and, most probably, very puerile way. The more he thought about this the more he changed his naturally full-chested delivery to a more reasonable and meek version designed to affront no one and to get as quickly to the end as he could.

The meeting ended, the room cleared and our colleague collected his notes. Being the last to leave he took advantage of checking the left over notepads for some clues. There, was the very piece of guilty paper that has caused him so many minutes of consternation. It was not possible to resist seeing the devilish comments that had been written about him. But as these things often turn out, he was left not knowing whether to be flatly disappointed or mightily relieved. On the paper it showed they had not been in any way preoccupied with him nor with anything apparently he had said. The note merely said, '*Your wife called. She says "It's 'Chicken Tonight' for dinner."*

Business is not a playground. We all worry about the numbers, work with statistics and, of course, we all need to. Making strong businesses even stronger requires some degree of measurement because, at the very least, the analytical sciences push us to re-examine things we may intuitively feel to be true – the phenomenon which, with enough chutzpah behind it, can miraculously transform opinions into mould-breaking ideas and products.

...being a beautiful business will become a hallmark of those who will be most successful at standing apart in the future.

The last word goes to the interviewees and their companies. How refreshing it is to hear the counterintuitive and wholly individualistic thinking from Jacques-Antoine Granjon, the founder of vente-privée, when he says, *"all that was invented by vente-privee wasn't done thinking about the customer. If I had created it according to customers, it never would have become vente-privee"*. Also, the apparently illogical but obviously smart deployment of 'strategic inconvenience', the limited information available to visitors to the vente-privee website that are not yet registered, helps maintain an element of value and preciousness for the brands and creates a feeling of discovery and intrigue for customers. As well as the final and wonderful deflation of the value of optimism, "You need to be a frustrated pessimist. A businessman who's too optimistic can be naïve. But naivety doesn't belong in a company because, to my way of thinking, only the paranoid survive. I am always paranoid and on the defensive. I have a motto, 'Capitolium saxo proxima' (A fall from grace can come quickly). You can be on the pinnacle like a powerful senator and then be hurled to a shameful death... from the very same place".

Here is a new perspective — paranoia and frustrated pessimism driving integrity, showing us just how real these hallmarks are in the lives of people in beautiful businesses. His comments are refreshing because they show how hard one has to think about the 'why' in business way before the measurement of the 'what'. Another of our chosen businesses stays with realism, with an honest appraisal of that overused word 'innovate' which has recently become a substitute for 'we can't think of anything original', from Tristram Carfrae at Arup. When we ask of any bold plans for the future, his response is characteristically defiant: "It's not going to be terribly exciting. Just more of the same thing. It's a dull answer but we deliberately change slowly." If all companies were as dull as Arup, then might the world be a more enjoyable place in which to work?

Our book sets out to celebrate the dimensions of success that often transform businesses into legend, the narratives we remember, recount, and amplify as we re-tell the story of our great moments in business. And the point is, we always remember them because we are fundamentally interested in what interests people.

Where to next?

Does this book herald a new view of the future for business? Beautiful business aren't exclusively linked to any single era — the book has many examples of noble and mature giants who have endured through generations. Perhaps it is fair to say, on the basis of what people have told us while writing this book, being a beautiful business will become a hallmark of those who will be most successful at standing apart in the future. We could speculate about the consequences of this in terms of branding, but it is safer to say that after all these years of close examination of numbers and metrics measuring the strength of the idea, we now need to turn our attention back to the creative idea itself.

What companies like BMW, Dr Irina Eris, Condé Nast, Rapha, Oticon, Rabobank, Arup, Opower, Egg energy, and 3M have shown us is that doing business in a certain way, imbued with human values, is the right way. And that this is about individuality, whether in large or small companies, mature giants or fledgling start-ups, Western or rapidly developing economies.

This book is a challenge to us to put into practice some of the ideas and ideals we have written about. This applies as much to our own business as it does to our clients and their businesses. It's the start of a different discussion about business. We relish this.

Endnotes

Introduction

1. *GE`s Ecomagination Reaches $105 Billion in Revenue (2012)* [Internet]. New York: Thomson Reuters. Available from: <uk.reuters.com/article/2012/06/28/idUS208085+28-Jun-2012+BW20120628> [Accessed 05/12/12].

2. Cadoche, G. (1989) *The Influence of Age and Ethanol on Parkinson's Disease* Thesis. Montpellier 1 University.

3. Cameron, W. B. (1963) *Informal Sociology: A Casual Introduction to Sociological Thinking.* New York: Random House.

4. Halberstam, D. (1993) *The Best and the Brightest.* New York: Ballantine Books.

5. Nehamas, A. (2001) *A Promise of Happiness: The Place of Beauty in a World of Art* [Internet] Connecticut: Yale University. Available from: <tannerlectures.utah.edu/lectures/documents/Nehamas_02.pdf> [Accessed 05/12/12].

6. *India Price to Book* (2012) [Internet]. Valuation Charts. VectorGrader.com. Available from: <vectorgrader.com/indicators/india-sensex-price-book> [Accessed 05/12/12].

Integrity

7. Drucker, P. F. (1974) *Management: Tasks, Responsibilities, Practices.* Oxford: Butterworth-Heinemann.

8. Gneezy, U. & Rustichini, A. (2000) *A Fine Is a Price. The Journal of Legal Studies.* [Internet]. Jan. Vol. 29, No. 1. pp. 1-17. Available from: <socio.ethz.ch/education/fs12/envirsoc/Gneezy_Rustichini_A_fine_is_a_price.pdf> [Accessed 05/12/12].

9. Employee Engagement Report 2011 – *Beyond the numbers: A Practical Approach for Individuals, Managers and Executives* (2011) [Internet] New Jersey: Blessing White Inc. Available from: <blessingwhite.com/eee_report.asp [Accessed 05/12/12].

10. Miller, P. (2006) *Multichannel Marketing, The Patagonia Way.* [Internet]. Philadelphia: Retail Online Integration. Available from: <retailonlineintegration.com/article/multichannel-marketing-the-patagonia-way-39064/1> [Accessed 05/12/12].

11. Casey, S. (2007) *Patagonia: Blueprint for Green Business* [Internet]. CNN Money. Chicago: Cable New Network. Available from: <money.cnn.com/magazines/fortune/fortune_archive/2007/04/02/8403423/index.htm> [Accessed 05/12/12].

12. Lowe, S. & McArthur, A. (2008) *Is It Just Me or is Everything Shit?* The Encyclopaedia of Modern Life. London: Hachette Digital.

13. Motavalli, J. (2012) *Comeback Companies* [Internet]. Texas: Success Magazine. Available from: <success.com/articles/print/1738> [Accessed 05/12/12].

14. Mfonobong, N. (2011) *5 Machiavellian Business Lessons From Billionaire Aliko Dangote* [Internet]. New York: Forbes.com LLC. Available from: <forbes.com/sites/mfonobongnsehe/2011/07/13/5-machiavellian-business-lessons-from-billionaire-aliko-dangote/> [Accessed 05/12/12].

15. Ahmed, A. S. et al. (2009) *How Costly is the Sarbanes Oxley Act? Evidence on the Effects of the Act on Corporate Profitability.* [Internet] Social Science Research Network: Tomorrow's Research Today. New York: Social Science Electronic Publishing, Inc. Available from: <papers.ssrn.com/sol3/papers.cfm?abstract_id=1480394> [Accessed 05/12/12].

16. Keifer, S. (2011) *What Zappos.com can teach us about the Supply Chain.* Gxsblogs 15 February [Internet blog]. Available from: <gxsblogs.com/keifers/2011/02/what-zappos-com-can-teach-us-about-the-supply-chain.html> [Accessed 05/12/12].

17. Carando, G. (2011) *Domino's Pizza Turnaround.* Psucomm473 20 October [Internet blog]. Available from: <psucomm473.blogspot.co.uk/2011/10/dominos-pizza-turnaround.html> [Accessed 05/12/12].

18. *Nissan posts record profit in fiscal 2000* (2001) [Internet]. Business News. Tokyo: The Japan Times Available from: <japantimes.co.jp/text/nb20010518a1.html> [Accessed 05/12/12].

19. Benjamin, T. (2005) *Carlos Ghosn: Nissan's Turnaround Artist* [Internet]. World Business. Chicago: Cable New Network. Available from: <edition.cnn.com/2005/BUSINESS/04/20/boardroom.ghosn/> [Accessed 05/12/12].

20. Ghosn C. & Riès P. (2005) *Shift: Inside Nissan's Historic Revival.* New York: Random House.

21. *Foundation Fact Sheet* (2012) [Internet]. Seattle: Bill & Melinda Gates Foundation. Available from: <gatesfoundation. org/about/Pages/foundation-fact-sheet.aspx> [Accessed 05/12/12].

22. Eisenberger et al. (2001) *Reciprocation of Perceived Organizational Support. Journal of Applied Psychology.* [Internet]. Vol.86 (1) pp.42-51. Washington DC: American Psychological Association Inc. Available from: <psychology. uh.edu/faculty/Eisenberger/files/05_Reciprocation_of_ Perceived_Organizational_Support.pdf> [Accessed 05/12/12].

Curiosity

23. *Iranians Mark National Day of Ferdowsi* (2011) [Internet]. Culture. Tehran: Fars News Agency. Available from: <english. farsnews.com/newstext.php?nn=9002250426> [Accessed 05/12/12].

24. Global Market Research 2011 (2011) [Internet] *An ESOMAR Industry Report in cooperation with KPMG Advisory. The Netherlands: ESOMAR.* Available from: <esomar.org/web/ research_papers/book.php?id=2253> [Accessed 05/12/12].

25. Ries, A & Trout, J. (2001) *Positioning: The Battle for Your Mind.* Chicago: R. R. Donnelley & Sons.

26. *Data, data everywhere* (2010) [Internet]. Special Reports. London: The Economist Newspaper Limited. Available from: <economist.com/node/15557443> [Accessed 05/12/12].

27. McAllister, H. C. (2012) *Estimate the Number of Grains of Sand on all the Beaches of the Earth.* [Internet]. Mano: University of Hawaii. Available from: <hawaii.edu/suremath/jsand.html> [Accessed 05/12/12].

28. Adams, C. (1982) *Schroedinger's Cat.* [Internet]. Chicago: Sun-Times Media, LLC. Available from: <straightdope.com/ columns/read/113/the-story-of-schroedingers-cat-an-epic-poem> [Accessed 05/12/12].

29. *Albert Einstein quotes* (2012) [Internet]. ThinkExist. Available from: <thinkexist.com/quotation/imagination_is_more_ important_than_knowledge-for/260230.html> [Accessed 05/12/12].

30. Napoleon H. (2005) *Think and Grow Rich.* Minnesota: Filiquarian Publishing LLC

31. Sneider, M. (2005) [Internet] *AcuPOLL White Paper: Pay Attention To The Details Or Your New Product Will Die A Slow, Painful Death.* North America: AcuPOLL. <brandchannel. com/images/papers/132_product_launch.pdf> [Accessed 05/12/12].

32. Hu, Y. (2012) The Paypal Mafia. Thinkhard-ly 4 August. [Internet blog]. Available from: <thinkhard-ly.com/1/ post/2012/04/the-paypal-mafia.html> [Accessed 05/12/12].

33. Bryant, A. (2011) *Fostering a Culture of Dissent* [Internet]. Business. New York: The New York Times. Available from: <nytimes.com/2011/07/17/business/david-sacks-of-yammer-on-fostering-dissent-corner-office.html?pagewanted=all> [Accessed 05/12/12].

34. Peck G. (1950) *Fattening for the Kill* [Internet]. Oregon: Heppner Gazette Times. Available from: <news.google.com/ newspapers?nid=1025&dat=19500323&id=hdokAAAAIBAJ &sjid=QxAGAAAAIBAJ&pg=2444,2578381> [Accessed 05/12/12].

35. Lowenstein, R.A. (1989) *Wild Ducks* [Internet]. Business. New York: The New York Times. Available from: <nytimes. com/1989/05/07/business/l-wild-ducks-048289.html> [Accessed 05/12/12].

36. *3M Aluminum Conductor Composite Reinforced: More Amps – What ACCR Is and How It Works* (2012) [Internet] US: 3M. Available from: <solutions.3m.com/wps/portal/3M/en_US/ EMD_ACCR/ACCR_Home/ProductBenefits/MoreAmps/> [Accessed 05/12/12].

37. Woodfill, J. (2000) *Origin of Apollo 13 Quote: "Failure is not an Option."* [Internet]. Available from: <spaceacts.com/ notanoption.htm> [Accessed 05/12/12].

38. *Quotations by Subject: Failure* (2012) [Internet]. Quotations Page. Available from: <quotationspage.com/subjects/ failure/> [Accessed 05/12/12].

39. Lepore, M. (2011) *Google's Marissa Mayer Says Failure is Fine But Do It Fast* [Internet]. Chicago: Alloy Digital. Available from: <thegrindstone.com/mentor/googles-marissa-mayer-says-failure-is-fine-but-do-it-fast-993/> [Accessed 05/12/12].

40. Whittaker, J. (2012) *Google is now just an ad company* [Internet]. London: Associated Newspapers Ltd. Available from: <dailymail.co.uk/sciencetech/article-2115393/Google-ad-company-Departing-exec-James-Whittakers-Goldman-Sachs-style-rant.html> [Accessed 05/12/12].

41. *Deep Thoughts - Innovation and Success - Perseverance vs. Futility* (2012) [Internet]. Government of Alberta. Available from: <agric.gov.ab.ca/$department/newslett.nsf/all/snack20132> [Accessed 05/12/12].

Elegance

42. Benzoni, G. (2005) *History of the New World*. USA: Adamant Media Corporation

43. Doyle, A. C. (1901) *The Hound of the Baskervilles*, London: George Newnes Ltd.

44. Symonds, M. (2010) *Teaching Business Leadership As Fine Art* [Internet]. Entrepreneurs. New York: Forbes.com LLC. Available from: <forbes.com/2010/10/22/business-school-fine-arts-leadership-careers-education.html> [Accessed 05/12/12].

45. Symonds, M. (2010) *Teaching Business Leadership As Fine Art* [Internet]. Entrepreneurs. New York: Forbes.com LLC. Available from: <forbes.com/2010/10/22/business-school-fine-arts-leadership-careers-education.html> [Accessed 05/12/12].

46. Eisner, E. W. (2002) *What Can Education Learn from the Arts about the Practice of Education?* [Internet]. California: *The Encyclopedia of Informal Education*, Available from: <infed.org/biblio/eisner_arts_and_the_practice_of_education.htm> [Accessed 05/12/12].

47. Naghshineh, S. et al. (2008) Formal Art Observation Training Improves Medical Students' Visual Diagnostic Skills. *Journal of General Internal Medicine*. Volume 23. Pp.991-997.

48. *2012 CEO Survey* (2012) [Internet]. Inc. 5000. New York: Mansueto Ventures LLC Available from: <inc.com/magazine/201209/inc-staff/survey-of-inc-500-ceos-how-they-work.html> [Accessed 05/12/12].

49. McDonald, D. (2012) *America's Most Inspiring CEOs* [Internet]. Features. New York: Hearst Communications. Available from: <esquire.com/features/most-inspiring-ceos-1012#slide-11> [Accessed 05/12/12].

50. Merrill, B. (2010) *Press Releases* [Internet] Arlington VA: Opower. Available from: <opower.com/company/news-press/press_releases/11> [Accessed 05/12/12].

51. Pick, F. (1916) *Lecture to the Edinburgh branch of the Design and Industries Association*. Life and Times of the London Underground Map: The London Underground Font. London: BBC MMII. Available from: <news.bbc.co.uk/dna/place-lancashire/plain/A673517> [Accessed 05/12/12].

52. Pick, F. (1936) The Organisation of Transport. *Journal of the Royal Society of Arts*, Vol 84, No 4337. 3 January. Pp. 207-221

53. Hotelling, H. (2006) Stability in Competition. *The Economic Journal* [Internet]. 11/11. Vol. 39. No.153. Pp. 41-57. Available from: <people.bath.ac.uk/ecsjgs/Teaching/Industrial%20Organisation/Papers/Hotelling%20-%20Stability%20in%20Competition.pdf> [Accessed 05/12/12].

54. Friedman, V. (2012) *Lunch with the FT: Peter Marino* [Internet]. Life & Arts: Food & Drink. New York: The Financial Times Limited. Available from: <ft.com/cms/s/2/56b940d4-07ef-11e2-9df2-00144feabdc0.html#axzz29O3sBBT8> [Accessed 05/12/12].

55. Larroca, A. (2012) *Peter Marino, the Leather Daddy of Luxury* [Internet]. The Cut. New York: New York Media LLC Available from: <nymag.com/thecut/2012/08/peter-marino-knows-how-to-design-stores.html> [Accessed 05/12/12].

56. Popova, M. (2012) *Cultural History Gem: Saul Bass's Original Pitch for the Bell Systems Logo Redesign, 1969.* [Internet]. New York: Brain Pickings. Available from: <brainpickings.org/index.php/2012/07/23/saul-bass-bell-logo-pitch-1969/> [Accessed 05/12/12].

57. Bass, J. and Kirkham, P. (2011) *Saul Bass: A life in Film & Design*. London: Laurence King

58. Postrel, V. (2003) *The Substance of Style: How the Rise of Aesthetic Value is Remaking Commerce, Culture, and Consciousness*. New York: HarperCollins Publishers Inc.

59. *Paul Rand quotes* (2012) [Internet]. ThinkExist. Available from: <thinkexist.com/quotation/without-aesthetic-design-is-either-the-humdrum/388595.html> [Accessed 05/12/12].

60. Waldmeir, P. (2012) *Haier seeks to boost European sales* [Internet]. Companies: Retail & Consumer. Qingdao: The Financial Times Limited. Available from: <ft.com/cms/s/0/d0ab49ba-b2b2-11e1-9bd6-00144feabdc0.html#axzz29YTxL6Iw> [Accessed 05/12/12].

61. *Gary Kasparov vs. The World* (2009) [Internet]. California: Chess.com. Available from: <chess.com/forum/view/game-showcase/gary-kasparov-vs-the-world2> [Accessed 05/12/12].

62. Nielsen, M. (2007) Kasparov versus the World. *michaelnielsen.org 21 August* [Internet blog]. Available from: <michaelnielsen.org/blog/kasparov-versus-the-world/> [Accessed 05/12/12].

63. *A Journey Through Time* (2011) [Internet]. Illy, in Brief: History. Trieste: Illy caffè Spa. Available from: <illy.com/wps/wcm/connect/en/company/illycaffe-history> [Accessed 05/12/12].

64. Neate, R. (2011) *Andrea Illy: Family Businessman Who's Raising the Bar for Premium Coffee* [Internet]. Business: The Friday Interview. London: Guardian News and Media Limited. Available from: <guardian.co.uk/business/2011/sep/22/interview-andrea-illy> [Accessed 05/12/12].

65. Kollewe, J. (2012) *Robert Hiscox to Bow out of Insurer After 43 Years at Helm* [Internet]. Business: Hiscox. London: Guardian News and Media Limited. Available from: <guardian.co.uk/business/2012/feb/27/robert-hiscox-bow-out-insurer> [Accessed 05/12/12].

66. Valladares, D. (2012) Truth, half lies and downright dishonesty. *Advertising Matters. 15th May* [Internet blog]. Available from: <advertisingmatters.blogspot.co.uk/2012/05/truth-half-lies-and-downright.html> [Accessed 05/12/12].

67. Spauwen, I. (2012) *Brand performance check report: KTC Limited* [Internet] Amsterdam: Fair Wear Foundation. Available from: <ktcquality.com/download/PDF/China%20-%20KTC%20Heshan%20Rondor%20-%20Apr%202012.pdf> [Accessed 05/12/12]

68. Ricardo Semler (2012) [Internet wiki]. Available from: <en.wikipedia.org/wiki/Ricardo_Semler> [Accessed 05/12/12].

69. LaBarre, P. (2012) Forget Empowerment—Aim for Exhilaration. managementexchange.com 25 April [Internet blog]. Available from: <managementexchange.com/blog/forget-empowerment-aim-exhilaration> [Accessed 05/12/12].

70. Hirokata, T., Osono E. & Shimizu N. (2008) The Contradictions that Drive Toyota's Success. *Harvard Business Review: The Magazine* [Internet] June. pp. 96-104. Available from: <hbr.org/2008/06/the-contradictions-that-drive-toyotas-success/ar/1> [Accessed 05/12/12].

71. Bubbles and Bling (2006) [Internet]. Intelligent Life. London: The Economist Newspaper Limited. Available from: <economist.com/node/6905921> [Accessed 05/12/12].

72. *Jay-Z Launches Cristal Bubbly Boycott* (2006) [Internet]. Today: Celebrities. New York: NBC News. Available from: <today.msnbc.msn.com/id/13350034/ns/today-entertainment/t/jay-z-launches-cristal-bubbly-boycott/#.UIUWeI73Ay4> [Accessed 05/12/12].

73. *Cristal 2002* (2002) [Internet]. Reims: Louis Roederer Champagne. Available from: <champagneroederer.com/modules/fiches_techniques/pdf/en/cristal_2002.pdf> [Accessed 05/12/12].

74. Barrett, T. (2000) About Art Interpretation for Art Education. *Studies in Art Education* [Internet] Autumn, Vol. 42, No. 1, pp. 5-19 <terrybarrettosu.com/pdfs/Barrett%20(2000)%20About%20Art%20Interpretation%20for%20Art%20Education.pdf> [Accessed 05/12/12].

Craft

75. Frankfurt, H. (2005) *On Bullshit*. New Jersey: Princeton University

76. *FournaiseTrack - Media Releases.* (2012) [Internet] USA: The Fournaise Marketing Group. Available from: <fournaisegroup.com/CEOs-Do-Not-Trust-Marketers.asp> [Accessed 05/12/12].

77. The quote popularly featured in 'No Logo' by Naomi Klein, p.9. According to Klein's footnote, the quote is originally from a Yumiko Ono article in the WSJ, titled 'Marketers see the 'naked' truth in consumer psyches', published 30/05/97

78. *KPMG Europe Annual Report* (2011) KPMG Europe LLP

79. *JP Morgan Chase & Co Annual Report* (2011) Tampa: JP Morgan Chase & Co

80. *Old Mutual Annual Report* (2011) London: Old Mutual plc

81. Steel, E. (2012) *Bleak Forecast for Global Ad Spend* [Internet]. Companies: Media. New York: The Financial Times Limited. Available from: <ft.com/cms/s/0/911f47f0-d261-11e1-abe7-00144feabdc0.html#axzz23VkFMTFb> [Accessed 05/12/12].

82. *Egypt: GDP* (2012) [Internet]. The World Fact Book: Africa. USA: CIA. (Available from: <cia.gov/library/publications/the-world-factbook/geos/eg.html> [Accessed 05/12/12].

83. *What is Sugru?* (2012) [Internet]. About. London: FormFormForm Limited. Available from: <sugru.com/about> [Accessed 05/12/12].

84. *Cyclist's Closet: Rapha's Women's Performance Roadwear + Giveaway* (2011) [Internet] Cycle and Style. Available from: <cycleandstyle.com/2011/11/cyclists-closet-raphas-womens-performance-roadwear-giveaway/> [Accessed 05/12/12].

85. *Team Sky* (2012) [Internet] London: Rapha. Available from: <rapha.cc/teamsky/> [Accessed 05/12/12].

86. *Facts and Figures* (2005) [Internet]. Tokyo: Mitsubishi Motors Corporation. Available from: <mitsubishi-motors.com/corporate/ir/share/pdf/e/fact2005.pdf> [Accessed 05/12/12].

87. Salkever, A. (2004) *John, Paul, George, Ringo...and Steve?* [Internet]. Bloomberg Businessweek. New York: Bloomberg L.P. Available from: <businessweek.com/stories/2004-09-29/john-paul-george-ringo-dot-dot-dot-and-steve> [Accessed 05/12/12].

88. Roberts, L. (2010) *Apple vs Apple: Long-Running Legal Dispute Delayed Beatle's iTunes Deal* [Internet]. Culture: Music: Music News. London: Telegraph Media Group Limited. Available from: <telegraph.co.uk/culture/music/music-news/8136469/Apple-vs-Apple-long-running-legal-dispute-delayed-Beatles-iTunes-deal.html> [Accessed 05/12/12].

89. *Apple leads U.S. retailers in sales per square meter* (2011) [Internet]. Tech-SEMAGAN. Available from: <french.gadgetmeet.com/apple-leads-u-s-retailers-in-sales-per-square-meter/> [Accessed 05/12/12].

90. *Loom Speed* (2012) [Internet]. Available from: <cantonbee.com/ExpoBee/Showroom/Content/Category.aspx?SRCID=30818260&pgn=1&pt=0> [Accessed 05/12/12].

91. *Satoshi Suzuki (Loopwheeler) Interview* (2008) [Internet]. Collingwood: Sneaker Freaker. Available from: <sneakerfreaker.com/articles/Nike-Loop-Wheel-Interview/> [Accessed 05/12/12].

92. Ogilvy, D. (1983) *Ogilvy on Advertising*. London: Prion Books Ltd.

93. Wheeler, D. (2012) *Signing Off: The Slow Death of the Signature in a PIN-Code World* [Internet]. Tech. Washington DC: The Atlantic Monthly Group. Available from: <theatlantic.com/technology/archive/2012/01/signing-off-the-slow-death-of-the-signature-in-a-pin-code-world/251934/> [Accessed 05/12/12].

94. *Gore Vidal Quotes: 26 of the Best* (2012) [Internet]. Culture: Books. London: Guardian News and Media Limited. Available from: <guardian.co.uk/books/2012/aug/01/gore-vidal-best-quotes> [Accessed 05/12/12].

95. *About The Economist Online* (2012) [Internet]. About Us. London: The Economist Newspaper Limited. Available from: <economist.com/help/about-us#About_Economistcom> [Accessed 05/12/12].

96. *Review of NK Saluhall* (2012) [Internet]. Destinations: Stockholm Shopping. New Jersey: John Wiley & Sons, Inc. Available from: <frommers.com/destinations/stockholm/S34517.html> [Accessed 05/12/12].

97. *NK (Nordiska Kompaniet), Stockholm* (2012) [Internet]. Stockholm: Shopping. Paris: Condé Nast. Available from: <concierge.com/travelguide/stockholm/shopping/18099> [Accessed 05/12/12].

98. Clifford, S. & Creswell, J. (2009) *At Bloomberg, Modest Strategy to Rule the World* [Internet]. Media & Advertising: Business. New York: The New York Times. Available from: <nytimes.com/2009/11/15/business/media/15bloom.html?_r=1&pagewanted=2> [Accessed 05/12/12].

99. Hass, N. (1995) *The House that Bloomberg Built* [Internet]. Features. New York: Mansueto Ventures LLC. Available from: <fastcompany.com/26334/house-bloomberg-built> [Accessed 05/12/12].

Prosperity

100. *America's Most Admired Companies: Steve Jobs Speaks Out* (2008) [Internet]. CNN Money. Chicago: Cable News Network. Available from: <money.cnn.com/galleries/2008/fortune/0803/gallery.jobsqna.fortune/4.html> [Accessed 05/12/12].

101. Woods, B. (2012) *New RIM Chief: BlackBerry must Chase Consumers* [Internet]. Topic: Tech Industry. London: CBS Interactive. Available from: <zdnet.com/new-rim-chief-blackberry-must-chase-consumers-3040094887/> [Accessed 05/12/12].

102. Steiner, C. (2011) *The Most Annoying Business Jargon* [Internet]. Entrepreneurs. New York: Forbes.com LLC. Available from: <forbes.com/2011/01/06/annoying-business-jargon-entrepreneurs-business_slide_2.html> [Accessed 05/12/12].

103. O'Connell, P. (2005) *Online Extra: Pierre Omidyar on "Connecting People"* [Internet]. Bloomberg Businessweek Magazine. New York: Bloomberg L.P. Available from: <businessweek.com/stories/2005-06-19/online-extra-pierre-omidyar-on-connecting-people> [Accessed 05/12/12].

104. *Etsy is the world's handmade marketplace.* (2012) [Internet]. About Etsy. New York: Etsy Inc. Available from: <etsy.com/about?ref=ft_about> [Accessed 05/12/12].

105. *Etsy is the world's handmade marketplace.* (2012) [Internet]. Press. New York: Etsy Inc. Available from: <etsy.com/press> [Accessed 05/12/12].

106. H.M. (2012) Outsourcing is so Last Year. *Babbage: Science and Technology. 11 May* [Internet blog]. Available from: <economist.com/blogs/babbage/2012/05/future-customer-support> [Accessed 05/12/12].

107. Tuttle, B. (2012) *Should We Stop Referring to People as 'Consumers'?* [Internet]. Psychology of Money. New York: Time Inc. Available from: <moneyland.time.com/2012/04/18/should-we-stop-referring-to-people-as-consumers/#ixzz26qOL47TB> [Accessed 05/12/12].

108. *Paul Polman: 'The power is in the hands of the consumers'* (2011) [Internet]. Guardian Sustainable Business. London: Guardian News and Media Limited. Available from: <guardian.co.uk/sustainable-business/unilever-ceo-paul-polman-interview> [Accessed 05/12/12].

109. Lewis, J.S. (1907) *John Lewis Partnership - Our Founder* [Internet]. About: Our Founder. London: John Lewis Partnership. Available from: <johnlewispartnership.co.uk/content/dam/cws/pdfs/about%20us/our%20founder/Our_Founder_Dear_to_my_Heart_Speech.pdf> [Accessed 05/12/12].

110. Franklin, B. (1748) *Advice to a Young Tradesman* [Internet]. Yale: Yale University Press. Available from: <franklinpapers.org/franklin/framedVolumes.jsp> [Accessed 05/12/12].

111. *One Planet Living* (2012) [Internet]. Gland: WWF. Available from: <wwf.panda.org/what_we_do/how_we_work/conservation/one_planet_living/> [Accessed 05/12/12].

112. Singer, N. (2012) *Mission Control, Built for Cities* [Internet]. Business Day: Business. New York: The New York Times. Available from: <nytimes.com/2012/03/04/business/ibm-takes-smarter-cities-concept-to-rio-de-janeiro.html?_r=1&pagewanted=all> [Accessed 05/12/12].

113. Rometty, V. M. (2011) CEO's Letter [Internet] New York: IBM. Available from: <ibm.com/ibm/responsibility/2011/ceos-letter/> [Accessed 05/12/12].

114. *Allen & Overy Annual Review* (2011) London: Allen & Overy LLP

115. Hashiba, L. (2012) *Innovation in Well-Being – The Creation of Sustainable Value at Natura* [Internet]. Stories: M-Prize Winner. USA: Management Innovation Exchange. Available from: <managementexchange.com/story/innovation-in-well-being> [Accessed 05/12/12].

116. Callard, A. (2010) *Interview: The Contrarian, Professor Aneel Karnani* [Internet]. Mumbai: Intellecap Publication. Available from: <beyondprofit.com/interview-the-contrarian-professor-aneel-karnani/> [Accessed 05/12/12].

117. Eccles R., Ioannou I., & Serafeim G. (2011) The Impact of a Corporate Culture of Sustainability on Corporate Behavior and Performance [Internet] Working Knowledge: The Thinking that Leads. Boston: President and Fellows of Harvard College. Available from: <hbswk.hbs.edu/item/6865.html> [Accessed 05/12/12].

118. Murray, S., Rohwedar, M. & White, R.P. (2000) *Pilot Analysis of Global Ecosystems: Grassland Ecosystems* [Internet]. Washington DC: World Resources Institute. Available from: <pdf.wri.org/page_grasslands.pdf> [Accessed 05/12/12].

119. *Our Mission* (2012) [Internet]. Company: Deutsche Bank Global. Frankfurt: Deutsche Bank AG. Available from: <db.com/unitedkingdom/content/en/deutsche_bank_global.html> [Accessed 05/12/12].

120. *Our History* (2012) [Internet]. Herzogenaurach: PUMA SE. Available from: <about.puma.com/> [Accessed 05/12/12].

121. *Life Cycle Assessment of Different Shoe Packaging Design* (2012) [Internet]. Herzogenaurach: PUMA SE. Available from: <puma.com/pdfs/lca-report.pdf> [Accessed 05/12/12].

Featured businesses

We would like to thank all the people we interviewed for Business is Beautiful — it was a privilege to discuss our themes and ideas. Everyone involved was enthusiastic, generous and open with their time, giving real insights into their businesses.

3M

Founded in 1902, 3M provides innovative technology around the world; their portfolio includes iconic products such as the Post-it® and Scotch® Cellophane Tape.

We spoke to:
Dr Larry Wendling
The Global Research Laboratory's Vice President

3m.com

Arup

Arup is an independent global firm of designers, planners, engineers and consultants, founded in 1946.

We spoke to:
Tristram Carfrae
Head of Global Buildings Practice

arup.com

Autolib'

Autolib' is an electric car sharing service introduced in Paris in December 2011. The business aims to cut noise pollution and is a part of the shift in mobility for the future.

We spoke to:
Morald Chibout
CEO

autolib.eu

BMW and BMWi

BMWi represents visionary electric cars and mobility services, inspiring design and a new understanding of premium that is defined by sustainability.

We spoke to:
From BMW Corporate — Bill McAndrews, Vice President, Group Communications Strategy and Michael Rebstock, Head of Product Communications

From BMW i — Ulrich Kranz, Head of Project i, Benoit Jacob, Head of Design and Uwe Dreher, Head of Brand Management

bmw.co.uk
bmw-i.co.uk

Condé Nast

Magazine publisher Condé Nast was founded in 1909 and has achieved its distinctive iconic status by being based on three elements: quality, careful decision-making and the element of surprise.

We spoke to:
Xavier Romatet
CEO of Condé Nast France,

condenast.com

Dr Irena Eris

Dr Irena Eris is a cosmetics business, founded in Poland in 1983. It is internationally known for high quality products developed using rigorous scientific research.

We spoke to:
Dr Irena Eris
Founder

eris.pl

EGG-energy

Established in 2009, EGG-energy takes electric power and packages it into portable, rechargeable and affordable batteries for low-income African households.

We spoke to:
Jamie Yang
CEO and Founder

egg-energy.com

Icebreaker

Outdoor clothing business, Icebreaker was founded in 1994 and stands apart from competitors by being built on people's kinship with nature, rather than conquering it.

We spoke to:
Jeremy Moon
CEO and Founder

icebreaker.com

Interface

Interface is a sustainable manufacturer of flooring that was established in 1973. Their open approach to testing ideas is key to achieving the business' mission to have zero negative impact by 2020.

We spoke to:
Ramon Arratia
Sustainability Director

interface.com

KTC

Founded in 1971, KTC is a manufacturer of garments, textiles and accessories based in Hong Kong. The business has transformed the Made in China label into a mark of quality.

We spoke to:
Gerhard Flatz
Managing Director

ktcquality.com

Narayana Hrudayalaya Hospitals

Established in India, Narayana Hrudayalaya Hospitals are making quality healthcare affordable and available to the masses.

We spoke to:
Dr Devi Shetty
Founder

narayanahospitals.com

Opower

Opower takes energy data and makes it understandable by being engaging, clear and honest. They provide advice on energy efficiency to help save money and reduce carbon emissions.

We spoke to:
Jeremy Faro
Senior Director of Brand

opower.com

Oticon

Oticon is a hearing aid manufacturer based in Denmark and was founded in 1904. A deep understanding of the people it works with and works for is at the center of the business.

We spoke to:
Søren Nielsen
President

oticon.com

Pão de Açúcar

Brazilian retail group Pão de Açúcar puts taking care of people within the business and the community around the business at the heart of its success.

We spoke to:
Vitor Fagá
Executive Director of Corporate Relations

paodeacucar.com.br

Rabobank

Founded over 100 years ago in the Netherlands, Rabobank is an international financial service provider to autonomous local banks.

We spoke to:
Vincent Lokin
Head of Cooperative and Governance, and
Bouke de Vries
Head of Financial Sector Research

rabobank.com

Rapha

Rapha was established in 2004 and creates cycling clothing and accessories that blend style with optimum performance.

We spoke to:
Simon Mottram
Founder and CEO

rapha.cc

Story

Situated in New York, retail store, Story, takes pride in its presentation and emphasizes building valuable relationships within the community.

We spoke to:
Rachel Schechtman
Founder

thisisstory.com

Threadless

Threadless is an e-commerce business founded in 2000. The online community creates and chooses designs that are made into products.

We spoke to:
Jake Nickell Founder & Chief
Community Officer

threadless.com

vente-privee

vente-privee.com organises exclusive online flash sales for designer brands and focuses on special deals for members of the website.

We spoke to:
Jacques-Antoine Granjon
CEO

vente-privee.com

Zetter

The Zetter Hotel and its sister the Zetter Townhouse are stylish boutique hotels situated in Clerkenwell, London.

We spoke to:
Mark Sainsbury
Founder and co-owner

thezetter.com
thezettertownhouse.com

About the authors

Jean-Baptiste Danet
CEO, Dragon Rouge

An Anglophile who began his career at Philips, Jean–Baptiste is a passionate promoter of design's ability to rejuvenate business. Moving from electronics into the design industry in the late 1990's, he quickly became the architect for the transformation of Interbrand's European business, where he worked with the French designer Gerard Barrau on iconic retail brands such as FNAC and Sephora. More recently, Jean-Baptiste took the role of Global CEO of Dragon Rouge and today oversees the company's group of eight international offices from New York to Shanghai. Jean-Baptiste is a Co-President of the International Commission and a boardmember of Croissance Plus, the organisation of more than 300 business leaders and entrepreneurs in France. With a thirty-year career behind him, including leading major programs for many world-renowned brands, Jean-Baptiste is recognised for his work in the luxury brands sector.

Nick Liddell
Strategy Director, Dragon Rouge

Nick was one of Interbrand's youngest recruits into its brand valuation group in 2000 where his strategic skills enabled him quickly to assume the lead for much of Interbrand UK's consulting output. Nick joined the breakaway strategy company Clear where he further expanded his role to include an international remit and advised a wide variety of famous brand names on their next moves. Although a dedicated champion of left brain deductive processes, Nick is a passionate fan of pure creativity as seen in the kind of exciting intuitive design that speaks volumes in its own terms. His current role enables him to combine both interests where he works closely with design and strategy teams across Dragon Rouge to help enrich ideas and outputs. Nick authored Interbrand's 'Most Valuable Brands Study' and Clear's 'Brand Desire Index'.

Lynne Dobney
Director for Knowledge and Reputation, Dragon Rouge

Lynne has been a leading figure in the UK design industry for over thirty years. She spent the lion's share of her early career working with Sir John and Lady Sorrell to build the influential corporate design business Newell and Sorrell, feted for its work on the British Airways 'tailfins' project, which was itself made equally famous through Margaret Thatcher's public dislike of the design. Lynne has been a chair of the UK's Design Business Association and COO of Interbrand UK where she set up BrandChannel. She was a co-founder of The London Design Festival, now in it's eleventh year, and MD of the consultancy Fortune Street which she set up with Tony Allen. Lynne is a qualified business coach and today works on developing and articulating ideas inside Dragon Rouge and on client projects with an emphasis on internal culture.

Dorothy Mackenzie
Chairman, Dragon Rouge London

Dorothy co-founded Dragon Rouge in London over twenty years ago. A pioneer in promoting the integration of sustainability into brand thinking, she has written a range of books and reports around this theme, including Design for the Environment and Corporate Reputation – Does the Consumer Care. She was a keynote speaker at the Sustainable Brands conference 2012 in London and her appointments have included the UK Government Advisory Committee on Business and the Environment and the Prince of Wales' Business and the Environment Programme. In December 2012, Dorothy was appointed a Non Executive Director to the Board of the Carbon Trust.

Tony Allen
Group Director Corporate Branding, Dragon Rouge

Tony spent a large part of his early career travelling between Amsterdam where he moved to run one of Newell and Sorrell's biggest bank rebranding projects, and New York, where the company had a burgeoning office and assignments with clients such as IBM and PwC. He has worked at Interbrand and at his own consultancy Fortune Street, as well as McCann-Erickson working on Coca-Cola with the aim to modify British tea drinking habits. A contributing author of The Economist book, Brands and Branding, Tony's experience in repositioning, strategy and identity for brands in mergers and acquisitions and at virtually any time of change has led him to work in most major and developing markets and industry sectors. His clients include banks, law firms, industrials, airlines, technology and telecommunications businesses, pharmaceuticals and countries.

Acknowledgements

With thanks to everyone at Dragon Rouge for their input, ideas, enthusiasm, support and patience, including – (but not limited to):

Alain Brochec, Alain Schicklin,
Andrea Lebris, Anne Luneau, Arek Los,
Barbra Wright, Belinda Lau, Ben Lickfett,
Christian de Bergh, Delphine Cadoche, Didier
Paccoud, Eliza Preston, Eric Zeitoun, Fiona
Bennie, Dr Frank Chen, Ian Farnfield, Jigna
Chauhan, Jocelyne Henri, Joe Hale, John
Tanner, Jonathan Chajet, Kate Waddell,
Malgosia Leniarska, Marie-Therese Cassidy,
Melanie Gransart, Meyric Rawlings,
Nathalie Avron, Olivier Grenier, Olivier Vinet,
Patrick Veyssiere, Pearse McCabe,
Pierre Cazaux, Robert Soar, Sarah Kochling,
Sofia Jarnfors, Thomas Jauss,
Xavier Possamat

Dragon Rouge is a global design and innovation business. Founded in 1984 in France by Patrick Veyssiere and Pierre Cazaux , it is a leading independent network, combining local expertise and consumer knowledge with a global strategic vision of brand management.

Paris
Dragon Rouge France
32 rue Pagès
92150 Suresnes
France
T: + 33 1 46 97 50 00
F: + 33 1 47 72 05 03

London
Dragon Rouge London
1 Craven Hill
London, W2 3EN
United Kingdom
T: + 44 207 262 44 88
F: + 44 207 262 64 06

New York
Dragon Rouge USA
30 W 21st Street, 9th Floor
New York, NY 10010
USA
T: + 1 212 367 8800

Shanghai
Dragon Rouge Branding
(Shanghai) Co., Ltd.
Room 701, No 378, Wukang Road,
Xuhui District
Shanghai, P.R. China
T: +86 21 6433 2058
F: +86 21 6433 2059

Hong Kong
Dragon Rouge China limited
Unit 01, 22/F, 88 Hing Fat Street
Causeway Bay
Hong Kong
T: + 852 2512 1340
F: + 852 2512 1349

Hamburg
Dragon Rouge Germany
An der Alster 3,
20099 Hamburg
Germany
T: + 49 40 380 374 0
F: + 49 40 380 374 44

São Paulo
Dragon Rouge Brazil
Av. Engenheiro Luiz Carlos Berrini 1748
23rd floor
São Paulo - SP – Brazil
CEP 04571-000
T: + 55 11 2663 2630

Warsaw
Dragon Rouge sp. z o.o.
ul. Łowcza 26
02 - 955 Warszawa
Poland
T: + 48 22 651 84 20
F: + 48 22 651 84 21

Zurich
Dragon Rouge GmbH
Kornhausstrasse 49
8037 Zürich,
Switzerland
T: +41 (0)43 537 52 90
M: +41 (0)76 412 23 13